BRAND STORY

BRAND STORY

ralph, vera, johnny, billy, and other adventures in fashion branding

JOSEPH HANCOCK
Drexel University

FAIRCHILD BOOKS
NEW YORK

Executive Editor: Olga T. Kontzias

Acquisitions Editor: Joseph Miranda

Editorial Development Director: Jennifer Crane

Development Editor: Michelle Levy

Manuscript Development: Molly Morrison, Newgen North America

Associate Art Director: Erin Fitzsimmons

Production Director: Ginger Hillman

Associate Production Editor: Andrew Fargnoli

Copy Editor: Susan Hobbs

Cover Design: Erin Fitzsimmons

Cover Art: © Kurt Krieger/Corbis; Lisa Larsen/Time Life Pictures/Getty Images; Lisa Larsen/Time Life Pictures/Getty Images; Nora Bibel/laif/Redux; Getty Images/Gallo Images; Courtesy of The Advertising Archives; Courtesy of Fairchild Publications, Inc.

Library of Congress Catalog Card Number: 2007928952

ISBN: 978-1-56367-622-2

GST R 133004424

Printed in China

TP15

For my family,
Edward Augustyn,
Margaret Miller,
and little Ruby J.

Without them this book
would have not
been possible.

CONTENTS

CONTENTS

EXTENDED CONTENTS

FOREWORD

by Thom Browne

Branding, *identity*, and *marketing* have been practiced as ways to build a business since the Industrial Revolution and certainly play a crucial and important role in any business today. Whether a car, a soft drink, a store, or insurance, the image a product projects defines it and its company, whom it appeals to, and the associations it conveys to the consumer.

With the proliferation of consumer culture in the last few decades, branding and marketing have been taken to the extreme of creating a brand concept even before a product. This may work if short-term success is the goal. However, if the goal is building a business for the long term, the first and most important component is to have a good product. A good product is even better if it has a strong concept behind it and is made well. Branding, a crucial part of a business, follows after and must respond to a product's basic strengths.

While I have always recognized that branding and marketing are very important aspects in building a business, I did not set out to create a "brand." I simply wanted to make well-made, hand-tailored suits that would appeal to people who thought that tailored suits are what their grandfathers and fathers wore. The silhouette, the detailing, and the make of the suits I created were what I wanted to wear. I thought that there might be a few others out there who would like them as well. But I also knew that my suits would not be for everyone. I was prepared to accept that and still am.

Keeping that attitude required consistency and patience, two other key elements in building brand identity. Maintaining and guarding what one has established and believes in requires diligence and care. While it is important to listen to the responses of the consumer, one also needs to remember that it takes time for ideas to be understood. The evolution of a product or brand, moreover, is different from just dropping one idea in favor of another. Once a brand identity is established, it can be enhanced

FIGURE F.1 Thom Browne stands in front of his signature suits that represent his brand's image.

through evolution, but frequent changes can confuse the consumer.

In recent years, since I began presenting fashion shows and collaborating with other companies, I have continued to stress the role of brand identity. In my own collection I have taken the ideas behind the silhouette I created at the inception of my company further. The concept and the production of my shows underscore my intention to provoke the conventions of our society and how it views men's fashion. My collaboration with the Black Fleece by Brooks Brothers collection has allowed me to renew interest in an iconic, 190-year-old American brand. Both collections come from the same place, but my ideas serve and strengthen distinctively different brands. My own collections and these collaborations have not always been positively accepted, just as when I first started my business. But by maintaining my principles and developing them patiently I have been able to create a distinct brand identity. Like my own story, *Brand/Story: Ralph, Vera, Billy, Johnny, and Other Adventures in Fashion Branding* reinforces the ideas of how both established and new brands develop their own identities. It reinforces the notion that good design in mass-produced products ensures their continual growth and development.

PREFACE

In our industry, time is of the essence. It seems like the day a product arrives in a retail store it is already history and out of style. Like fashion, branding changes at the speed of light. It waits for nothing. Therefore, when we examine fashion branding, there has to be an understanding that what we are really viewing is history in the making. This book is not intended to be a history of fashion branding; however, because of the speed of fashion, it is inevitable.

Each of the chapters in this text describes a unique form of branding that has occurred. An objective of each reader should be to examine the chapters and then search out where each of these fashion brands is positioned in today's marketplace. Companies do not freeze in time, and these brands have not stood still since the writing and printing of these pages. However, what makes this book so valuable is that it presents a launching pad for each student or reader to understand how these brands evolved. It reveals their history, it discusses significant products, and most importantly, it reveals their strategy and positioning in the global market.

If, as you read this book, you go to the Web and search for their names to see what has happened since the production of this book, I am sure you will be surprised. Each of these brands continues to grow, reposition itself, and change. Always remember, it is people that "make or break" brands, whether they are consumers, merchandisers, fashion designers, store operations, managers, or sales people.

I hope this writing inspires you to become fascinated with both the visual spectacle and written dialect of branding that attempt to entice you to spend money and buy more products. Learn to analyze all brands as you read through this text. Enjoy!

Acknowledgments

This book would not have existed without the support of many people. First, I would like to thank Fairchild Books, especially Olga T. Kontzias, Joseph Miranda, Michelle Levy, Jennifer Crane, Andrew Fargnoli, Erin Fitzsimmons, and Jaclyn Bergeron, who have been so supportive of this project during its evolutionary process. Next, I would like to thank Molly Morrison for all her guidance during the writing and revision of the manuscript. In addition to all the editorial support, I would like to thank the Antoinette Westphal College of Media Arts & Design at Drexel University; the college of Fashion Design, Architecture, and Building at the University of Technology in Sydney, Australia; and the Centre for Fashion Studies in Stockholm, Sweden for financial support on this project, and for allowing me to spread my enthusiasm for branding with their students. Also, I would like to extend my personal gratitude to Ben Sander, Jason Sutherland, Reneé Thomas, Billy Curtis, Johnny Earle, Michelle Bakar, Sean Cole, Lynn McGrane, Krista Pharr-Lowther, Jill Roberts, Dante Pauels, Brini Maxwell, and Jennifer Lea Cohan for all the materials and time they contributed for this text. With much appreciation, I would like to acknowledge my colleagues, especially my lifelong mentor Dr. Patricia Cunningham, and Dr. Vicki Karaminas, Dr. Louise Wallenberg, Dr. Judy Miler, Gayle Strege, Ann Keith Kennedy, those who supported me in the Department of Design—and all of my friends (Sandi Wenger and Ernest Henry III) who had to listen to me talk for hours about this book and who shared their ideas on how it could be used in the classroom. I would like to thank the people whom Fairchild Books enlisted to review the first draft manuscript of this book for their time and their useful suggestions: Amy J. Harden Leahy, Ball State University; Pat Turner, Fashion Institute of Design & Merchandising; and Van Dyk Lewis, Cornell University. I would also like to thank the Antoinette Westphal Faculty Development Mini-Grant Program for financially supporting this project. Finally, I would like to say "thank you" to everyone for whom I have worked in my 20 years of retailing—you are the ones who molded my views on the importance of branding in the first place.

BRAND STORY

Modern eye

CHAPTER ONE

INTRODUCTION

WHAT IS FASHION BRANDING?

The Story Begins

We are what we buy, so for some of us fashion is a way to express identity. But how do we choose one brand to purchase over others? What makes some fashion brands more special than others? The communication between a particular clothing brand and the consumer is a special connection. Through some method, the retailer, manufacturer, or designer label reaches out and grabs an individual's interest.

I know that I, personally, respond to these methods when going out to buy a new product or even in finding a new doctor. For example, I chose my current optometrist's office, where I have my eyes examined and purchase glasses, as a result of its advertising. The establishment is called Modern Eye, located in Philadelphia, Pennsylvania. Modern Eye is a very hip, fun, and contemporary store that treats its customers like royalty. However, what really drew me to Modern Eye was the strong brand message. The nostalgia and sheer genius of its advertising logo, the Modern Eye Guy, created an instant connection for me as a customer because I understood the story that was presented in the ad. Plus, by using this strategy, Modern Eye created an awareness of the type of eyeglasses that it sells. I was not surprised to find that it carried hip brands such as Paul Smith, Oliver Peoples, and L.A. Eyeworks.

The Modern Eye ad features two icons of historical and cultural significance. The first is the muscle man. He represents a Charles Atlas type with his perfect gym body. Gym culture and bodybuilding played a key role in advertising during the twentieth century, and continues to do so today.

Most consumers can also relate on some level to the bathing beauties in the ad. Beauty pageants are universally familiar. So how does this humorous and extremely campy ad effectively serve the simple purpose of selling Modern Eye as the place to get your eyes examined in Philadelphia? The branding strategy has a logo (the Modern Eye Guy) and tells a great story using history and cultural symbols that most of us can understand. The story is reminiscent of the nostalgic Charles Atlas ads for bodybuilding in which the frail boy realizes that to "get women" he must work out and build his muscles. Modern Eye's ad resembles the last frame of the historical Atlas ads where the skinny boy is transformed into a muscle-bound hunk adorned by two bathing beauties. Modern Eye has turned these icons into a branding strategy that reflects a culture and elicits an emotional response from the viewer. Modern Eye has related to a specific market niche.

What Is Fashion Branding?

Fashion branding has been defined as "The *cumulative image* of a product or service that consumers quickly associate with a particular brand, it offers an overall experience that is unique, different, special and identifiable."[1] Branding is also "A *competitive strategy* that targets customers with products, advertising, and promotion organized around a coherent message as a way to encourage purchase and repurchase of products from the same company."[2] Branding is not just about individual products, but creates an identity for the company, for consumers, as well as for those who work within the organization. Branding creates a vision for the company. In addition to these concepts of fashion branding, *Brand/Story: Ralph, Vera, Johnny, Billy, and Other Adventures in Fashion Branding* focuses on the creation of a perception that is generated through *brand storytelling.*

Fashion branding is the context that surrounds the garment as well as the image that designers, retailers, manufacturers, and promotional consultants create in order to encourage consumers to buy new items. Fashion branding can make fashion seem fun, exciting, innovative, and unique; fashion brands need a solid identity to be understood by consumers. Fashion branding shapes and contextualizes a garment or accessory to establish its identity.

A T-shirt, pair of jeans, skirt, sweatshirt, khaki pants, baseball cap, and even a pair of shoes can be dull and indistinguishable without the help of fashion branding. Whereas couture garments rely on craftsmanship to sell, mass-produced products depend on branding to make them appear unique among their competitors. Branding has allowed mass-produced merchandise (even underwear!) to become an exciting fashion commodity sold in luxury markets (Figure 1.1). For example, Dolce & Gabbana has established itself as a luxury brand with an internationally recognizable reputation. Their logo appears on items ranging from designer handbags to cologne and perfume bottles; it has become iconic through mass merchandising. The design duo's reputation allows them to license their names for products such as fragrance, timepieces, kids' fashions, swimwear, and even men's underwear, lending luxury through their D&G division. Because Dolce & Gabbana is associated with high-quality luxury garments and style, the company is able to retail items at a higher-than-average price, such as men's underwear for $75 a pair.

The advertising medium, context, and style, should reflect the brand. For example, for luxury items, creating high-quality print advertising for a product leads to the perception of a brand like D&G as superior in fashionability and quality. In addition, the use of celebrity endorsement gives the appearance of higher status. In this ad, Dolce & Gabbana reinforces the brand by associating their product to the Italian men's soccer team, Nazionale, which could possibly connect to a new target market. Even though it is just a pair of pima cotton underwear, the designer name, brand image, and marketing strategy makes the product appear special.

Fashion branding is the process whereby designers, manufacturers, merchandisers, strategists, creative directors, retailers, and those responsible for selling fashion create campaigns and give fashion garments a unique identity. But branding is not just

FIGURE 1.1 Dolce & Gabbana underwear advertisement, 2007.

about the product; branding is also about creating a clear vision and strategy for a company. Branding gives everyone involved a clear direction and focus.

Although many people have written about brands, few have really examined fashion brands and looked at those who sell fashion brands as storytellers. The goal of this book is primarily to describe what goes into a fashion brand and to show how each featured company has developed a unique *story* for themselves and their product lines.

Fashion Branding and Storytelling

In their book, *Storytelling: Branding in Practice*, Klaus Fog, Christian Budtz, and Baris Yakaboylu describe storytelling as the means for a creating a brand. The storytelling process relies on a company's capability to make an emotional connection through their brand and to build target markets.[3] Fog et al. believe that a brand reaches full consumption potential when an emotional attachment to consumers is attained; when the consumers and employees of the brand are able to understand the company's values and messages. Storytelling is the vehicle that communicates these values in a process that is easy for consumers to understand. Storytelling speaks to the emotions of the target market, which in return becomes loyal to the company.[4]

Fog et al. describe how advertising reflects the basic concepts of storytelling, which they define as message, conflict, characters, and plot. Advertising uses this same formula and is able to pique consumer interest while building associations to their products and creating emotional meaning.[5] For example, Apple computers have continually recreated their brand through creative marketing. It seems that the whole basis for their branding concept is to create social and political communities.[6] Products such as a U2 limited edition iPod suggest Apple's identification with artists like Bono (and his fans). And a portion of the purchase price for a (PRODUCT) RED special edition iPod goes to the Global Fund to Fight AIDS in Africa. (PRODUCT) RED was created by Bono and his colleague Bobby Shriver.

Apple's "Are You a Mac or a PC?" campaign featured two individuals; one who pretends to be a Mac computer and the other who pretends to be a PC. Each individual tells a story about who they are and how they perform. However, what is crucial in the ad is the characters' appearance. Representing the PC is a nerdy overweight suit-wearing IBM executive-type, whereas a trim, young, attractive, jeans and sneaker-wearing hip young man signifies the Apple computer. The PC seems uptight and inefficient, whereas the Apple is relaxed and very efficient, thus building a social community in which "Apple people" are attractive, cool, and casual as well as efficient. Who would you want to be?

If you are still skeptical over the whole idea of storytelling as a means for brands to build their names for mass consumption,

FIGURE 1.2 The original Santa Claus created for the Coca-Cola Company in 1931.

then think Coca-Cola. This company reaches a global market and has created an iconic image with their red-and-white label that people around the world know as Coke. However, did you know that Coca-Cola is responsible for creating the familiar American Santa Claus in the red-and-white suit (Figure 1.2)? In 1931 Coca-Cola introduced the character and, by including him over the years in various poses, with elves, and in different scenarios, Coca-Cola not only generated stories about Santa, they actually co-branded him with their product. How's that for a great fashion story?!

A Passion for Brands

The goals of this book are to entertain, shock, educate, and enlighten you, building your passion for brands. To fully understand and apply the information, each chapter ends with discussion questions and an exercise.

The framework for this text comes from a cultural critical perspective. In other words, the goal is to question what each fashion brand is about, why the companies advertise the way they do, and to learn not to take advertisements and brands at face value. It is important to think analytically and learn to *read* advertisements, which clarifies the companies' intentions. In today's computerized world, everyone is spoon-fed information; this text is written in a manner that will encourage critical thinking. Students of fashion and consumers need to *think*: What does the biography of a company and its advertising say about that company? How does the company's message make consumers want to buy or not buy? Are the images that are created positive or negative? This text does not judge the fashion brands presented, but lets you decide for yourself. This author does suggest some opinions about particular brands; however, you will have your own ideas, too. All the fashion companies, interviewees, and editors who participated in the writing of this book encourage the readers to visit websites, sign up for mailing lists, and, of course, visit stores. In short, "Go outside!"

Although some texts try to quantify brands as a form of empirical research and scientifically explain the concept of fashion branding, this book refers to qualitative and semiological notions with regard to critical thinking. *Brand/Story: Ralph, Vera, Johnny, Billy, and Other Adventures in Fashion Branding* encourages participation in popular culture. As the reader, you will need to develop your knowledge about all fashion brands and the images they present in the media. So it is probably a good idea to supplement this book with magazines, such as *W*, *Vogue*, and *GQ*. When you read the chapters, refer to company websites, business periodicals, and other magazines to see what has happened at the company since this writing. You need to look at as many publications as possible in addition to the Internet; after all, it is in print where fashion branding is presented as artwork and is viewed by the average consumer.

Although some of the brands in this book could be considered a little risqué, I offer no apology. In the world of fashion merchandising there has been one tried-and-true motto . . . *sex sells*! I have chosen to use companies whose branding methods may be offbeat, and the accompanying visuals may seem shocking. But anyone who wants to work in fashion must be comfortable talking about sex.

Also, to keep consumers interested, many brands relate to various types of people. For this text the author exposes the reader to a diverse array of fashion brands that market to contemporary consumers. However, all will enjoy the past and current fashion brands featured in this text.

Discussion Questions

1. What is fashion branding? How does branding establish a product's identity?

2. How are companies able to sell items like T-shirts, jeans, and sunglasses at high prices? Can you give an example of another item sold in the luxury market that might not have been traditionally perceived as a luxury good?
3. Race, ethnicity, religion, and sexual orientation play a part in purchasing decisions. Identify three consumer groups that are different from you. In your opinion, do they differ from each other with regard to fashions and the types of brands they purchase? Why or why not?

Exercise

Find a fashion advertisement. Identify any historical, social, or cultural icons in the ad and share the story the ad is trying to tell the viewers. How does this ad make the consumer want to purchase the product?

Miles Davis wore khakis.
GAP
KHAKIS

CHAPTER TWO

THINKING CRITICALLY

A HISTORY OF FASHION BRANDS AND CULTURE

From Modern to Postmodern and Beyond

Fashion branding became important as the popularity of mass-produced fashion (or mass fashion) grew in the twentieth century. The development of mass media allowed fashion to diffuse through society. The growth in popularity of ready-to-wear and sportswear, and advances in manufacturing technologies, led to the quick design, production, and distribution of fashion at all social class levels. The theory of simultaneous adoption of fashions suggests that garments enter at all levels of the consumer market with variations in quality and price line in order to accommodate consumer spending. This allows each consumer to purchase and use a current style according to his or her interests and budget. Manufacturers and retailers catered to the middle class and lower-end markets by designing and producing garments for these more price-conscious consumers.[1] However, for their garments to achieve prominence, retailers and manufacturers had to adopt various methods of promotion targeting specific types of clientele. Mass marketing included advertising and fashion branding directed at all consumer groups. Figures 2.1

through 2.4 exemplify the "everyman" quality of advertising that was common in the first half of the twentieth century.

During what is known as the modern period (c.1890–1945), function and use value were emphasized in fashion.[2] Consumers were influenced by practicality, style, fabrication, and availability of products that were new to them.[3] Fashion branding focused on giving consumers the features (fabric, fit, color, style) and benefits (functionality) that were important to them. For example, it is simple to understand how underwear (see Figure 2.1) is useful, and the advertisements in Figures 2.2 through 2.4 suggest how each of those products could be used. The Burberry dress in Figure 2.3 demonstrates the product and its function by showing a young woman ice skating while wearing the dress. This ice-skating ad is a forerunner to the type of advertising that emphasizes context and placement of product as a key selling strategy. *Context*, as defined for this text, is the medium, circumstances, or situation in which the product and the message (the ad) are transmitted and received. For example, in Figure 2.3,

FIGURE 2.1 [LEFT] Advertisement for B.V.D. "coat cut undershirts and knee length drawers," circa 1910.

FIGURE 2.2 [RIGHT] Advertisement for Arrow Airtone shirts, 1929.

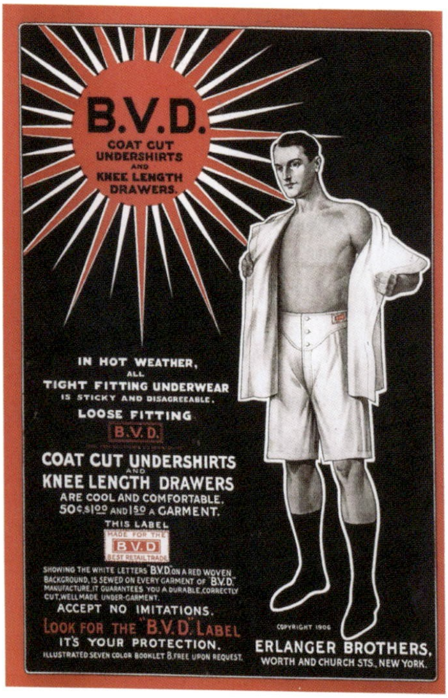

FIGURE 2.3 [LEFT] Burberry advertisement for its 1930s winter sports dress, showing both form and function.

FIGURE 2.4 [RIGHT] 1940s Air Step Shoes advertisement.

the context is the use of a print ad (medium) as well as the text and illustration within the ad. During this time the explosion of products from a vast array of manufacturers and retailers made branding a key visual means by which advertisers could demonstrate the features and benefits of products.

After World War II, technology, transportation, and mass communications rapidly improved as mass production increased. Returning from the war, veterans began to move into the suburbs to start families. Fashion retailers, manufacturers, and designers began to strategize about how they could benefit from this social trend. The mass markets began to grow, and consumers began spending more on products to attain an "American dream" lifestyle. The concept of "keeping up with the Joneses" became popular as consumers tried to outdo one another through home improvements, automobiles, and fashion. To capture this new consumer dollar, what became important for retailers, manufacturers, and designers was the inclusion of *meanings* and *lifestyle* in advertising to relate products to the American dream.

The circa 1950 Jantzen swimwear ad in Figure 2.5 exemplifies the type of ad that dominated the market at the time, creating excitement for simple products such as bathing suits. This ad presents the features and benefits of the bathing suit, but what is more important is the *meaning* emphasized by the model's expression (in addition to her big diamond earrings). Also the word *it* (as in Italy) suggest that Italy was the "it" place. The two other models show the rest of the swimsuit line and suggest alternative looks, so the viewer could envision how sexy she could be in this swimwear.

By inserting a set of manly hands into the photo, Jantzen alluded to the viewer that the woman who wore this suit would have the attention of the man she was with or wished to attain. The features of the swimsuit also added to the general perception of the garment as sexy; "shapemakery" (a built-in girdle) supplied the desired female form of the period. This Jantzen suit provided form and function to the consumer.

FIGURE 2.5 A Jantzen swimwear advertisement from the 1950s.

Postmodern Advertising

During the 1960s a fashion language of sorts was developed. According to French philosopher Roland Barthes, clothing garments are created and stylized in the design process to suit current fashion. Barthes believed that a garment is actually present in the fashion system at three distinct levels: the *real garment* or actual garment itself; the *terminological garment*, which signifies the word (e.g., T-shirt, jeans, blouse, cargo pants—basic terms, no adjectives) used to describe the object; and the *rhetorical written garment*, which includes how the clothing is described through words and photographed images (the fashion marketing), for example, Abercrombie & Fitch T-shirt, Diesel jeans, Armani blouse, J. Crew cargo pants. Barthes believed that the real garment was desired by the consumer; but as his studies helped scholars to understand, it is the rhetorical written garment's presentation in photographs (in which the garment is presented either as real or is manipulated to create a fantasy garment) that is more important for stimulating consumption.[4]

Jean Baudrillard, an influential theorist, defined *postmodernism* as a time of simulation in which the boundaries between what is real and what is perceived as real have been conflated. This conflation blurs the lines between what an individual knows as reality and what *is* reality, thus causing confusion.[5] This concept of an individual's inability to distinguish between what is real and attainable versus fantasy is what Baudrillard called *hyperreality*. Those having *social standing* (Baudrillard's words for people of cultural and social power; in this book, the people who create fashion brands) at the macro levels of consumer culture create the distortions between reality and hyperreality.[6] Baudrillard contended that the sign (the real or the image) is distorted by moving through the following four stages:

1. It is a reflection of basic reality.
2. It masks and perverts a basic reality.

3. It masks the *absence* of a basic reality.
4. It bears no relation to any reality whatsoever: It is its own pure simulacrum (simulation).[7]

In the first stage, the object is shown in what Baudrillard calls the natural state; for example, an item displayed alone without context or verbal or visual presentation. In stage two, the item is aesthetically presented in a contextual state with verbal and visual cues that have been created by those of social standing who distort the object and give it new meaning. Stage three represents the absence of all previous reality of the object. The origins, the use, histories, functions, and ideologies of a garment are erased by those of social standing; moreover, it is placed in a fantasy context. In stage four, the object is part of a whole new reality and has almost no relation to its origin. It is *hyperreal.*

Baudrillard believes hyperreality presents itself to consumers through media. Television, print advertising, computers, and other forms of communication create *surreal* life situations, but present them to consumers as *real.*[8] Airbrushed fashion models in magazines, bogus personal profiles on Internet dating services, and even distorted lenses on television cameras alter the real appearances of their subjects while alluding to the viewer that the subject is *natural.* For Baudrillard, the methods used by advertisers to sell products were examples of hyperreality, and branding reflected those notions.

Figure 2.6, a 1960s ad for Maidenform bras, is an excellent example of the beginnings of postmodern advertising. This ad illustrates sheer storytelling about the product. The viewer is not only drawn to the bra in the center of the photo, but also to the glamorous outfit of the woman, the trophies, the dog, and various other elements of the photo. This photo illustrates a context for selling Maidenform bras. After consumers see the bra, their eyes begin to wander and look at the other elements. Why is she holding that trophy? Why is there a dog in the photo? What is the ribbon under the dog for? Why is she wearing a cocktail dress? Perhaps she just entered her dog in a show and won first prize. Or maybe she won the talent competition in a beauty pageant by demonstrating dog tricks. Whatever the case, only after we read the text, "I dreamed I stole the show in my Maidenform bra," do we realize that the entire event is a dream and not real. It is total fantasy.

So, how is the fantasy transferred to a context such as a retail store, like Victoria's Secret (Figure 2.7)? How do the music, smell, sights, and sounds of the store influence an ultimate brand experience? And will the lingerie or undergarments purchased at Victoria's Secret have the same meaning after they leave the store? In other words, does the fantasy garment lose its appeal when the real garment is discovered?

Does the marketing slogan "What Is Sexy?" maintain its appeal in the average middle-class home, or does it change mean-

I dreamed I stole the show in my maidenform bra
CHANSONETTE®... best-loved Maidenform bra... now in care-free, iron-free Dacron*. Famous, fabulous combination of circular and spoke-stitched cups for superb fit, luscious curves. White, iced champagne, black. A,B,C cups, 2.50. D cup, 3.50.

FIGURE 2.6 A Maidenform bra ad from 1962 illustrates storytelling in advertising.

ing? Will every consumer look like the fantasy created in the window? The answers to these types of questions lead to a better understanding of fashion branding and the types of stories it relates to the viewer. Ads and window displays should not be accepted at face value by the student of fashion. Everything should be analyzed to encourage critical thinking. This was Baudrillard's goal through his critique of branding.

Postmodern Branding Semantics

Baudrillard believed that *brands* are the principal concepts of advertising culture, and that they constitute a new discourse in the order of consumption.[9] According to Baudrillard, "those of social standing have repackaged consumer products in hyperreal scenarios in order to generate continuous consumption."[10] In turn, those of social standing who use media to create advertising and marketing to sell products are influenced by postmodern popular culture and consumer lifestyles. Also, with the development of postmodern brand culture, ideas continue to surface; postmodern ideological concepts such as *fragmentation, de-differentiation, chronology,* and *pastiche* are applicable to current advertising campaigns. Postmodern theory and branding discourse assimilate into a contemporary vocabulary that is now considered everyday business semantics. Similarly, as Asa

FIGURE 2.7 Victoria's Secret store, Easton Towne Center, Columbus, Ohio.

Berger states in *The Portable Postmodernist*, "retailers, marketers, and branding executives incorporate postmodern concepts to create their own definitions and meanings of these terms."[11]

Fragmentation describes the separation of similar, mass-oriented groupings into smaller, specialized product ranges.[12] Moreover, mass-produced items are tailored to specific consumer segments. In retailing, terms such as *target market* or *market niche* describe the end result of fragmentation. These notions of fragmentation reflect a diverse marketplace in which each consumer's taste is unique and individualized.

De-differentiation suggests the blurring of high and low cultures. High culture refers to traditional art practices and what has previously been defined as art, such as sculptures and paintings. Low culture includes media such as fashion photography because it is used in advertising. These notions of high and low art and culture have been altered in the minds of consumers. New formats, such as graphic art and digital media, are now considered art as well.[13] With regard to fashion, the fuzzy line between fashion-as-art and art-as-fashion is a perfect example of de-differentiation. Gap and Abercrombie & Fitch commissioned renowned photographic artists Bruce Weber, Herb Ritts, and Albert Watson to shoot their pocket-Ts and denim. Advertising had not traditionally been viewed as high art, but some critics may have needed to expand their understanding of art after seeing these high-quality images.

For example, Figure 2.8 features pop singer Betty Boo in an ad for Gap's 1991 Individuals of Style campaign. The original concept of the campaign was to feature up-and-coming celebrities wearing a Gap T-shirt, jeans, or denim jacket. In most photos, like this one, the celebrity wore one garment that was Gap. This allowed the viewer to see how someone like Betty Boo incorporated Gap into her wardrobe. Before participating in this ad campaign, Betty Boo had released her CD *Boomania*, which made her an instant hit on the dance charts. Gap was a hot brand because of its use of rising stars like Betty Boo.

The Gap posters and ads became collectors' items because they had been created by photographers who were considered artists. Over time, however, this campaign's appeal has dwindled. The concept has been watered down. Well-known celebrities are now shown wearing complete Gap outfits rather than incorporating Gap into their individual style. However, the high-art status of the original Individuals of Style campaign has been validated by Gap through its release of the book *Individuals*, which is sold with its Product(Red) line.

The term *chronology*, as used by Baudrillard, refers to a consumer's preoccupation with nostalgia and an interest in the past. A consumer may become enchanted with finding what appears to be an original item.[14] Retailers appeal to these con-

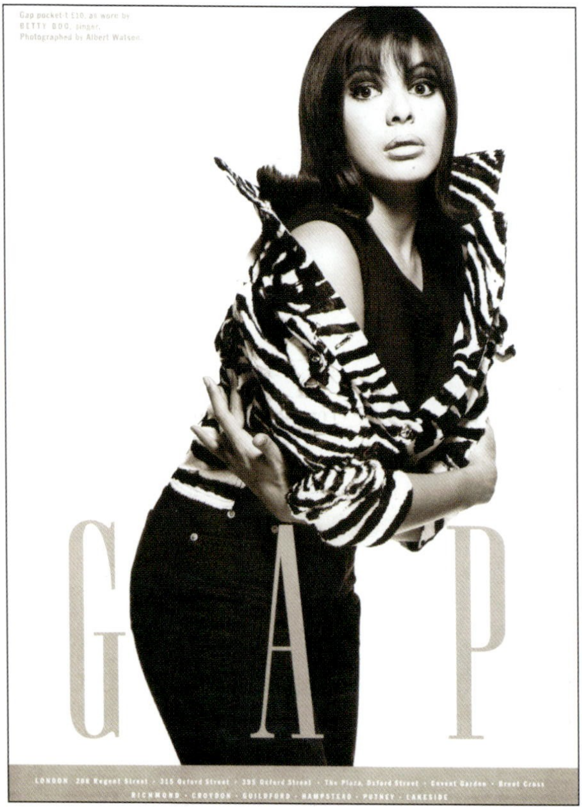

FIGURE 2.8 Gap's 1991 "Individuals of Style" campaign featured up-and-coming pop star, Betty Boo.

FIGURE 2.9 A 1973 U.K. advertisement for Hush Puppies touts the "genuine" handcrafted quality of the shoes.

sumers using terms such as *real*, *authentic*, and sometimes even *vintage*, to describe their products that are actually knock-offs or brand new. An example would be the 1973 Hush Puppies ad shown in Figure 2.9. Hush Puppies featured a nostalgic shoe-making process in the upper panels of the ad. This created a notion for the viewer that Hush Puppies were still produced by hand on a shoe cobbler's bench, when in reality they were mass produced. The branded message presented in this ad may have led the viewer to believe that Hush Puppies were *authentic* quality shoes, when in reality they were inexpensive versions of handmade footwear. Another word that marketing agents like to use it *genuine* (Genuine Hush Puppies Still Under a Fiver!), which implies authenticity and makes the consumer think he or she is getting a high-quality product. However, this ad is promoting a bargain and not necessarily quality.

However, Hush Puppies are an established brand and many consumers love the shoes. They are a great value for the price. Even today, Hush Puppies have had resurgence in the shoe market and have been retro-branded (reinvented as a new branded product with a contemporary twist). A consumer who buys Hush Puppies today may feel he or she is getting the original, authentic, or real Hush Puppies from the 1970s, but what he or she is really getting is a new pair of shoes that has been designed and produced using current manufacturing techniques. Over time, the authenticity of a nostalgic product fades. The product has to change and reinvent itself through time and context; however, many brands rely on retro branding to create a romanticized image of the brand.

Pastiche, as employed in Baudrillard's thesis, can be defined as a collage. In postmodern consumer culture, pastiche relates to the use of mixing traditional and nontraditional items in order to create a new context.[15] Actress Sharon Stone demonstrated postmodern fashion techniques when she wore a Gap turtleneck with an Armani couture jacket to the 70th annual Academy Awards. By mixing a mass fashion garment with couture, Stone created a postmodern look.

Fashion Branding: Connecting to Shoppers

The main function of fashion branding is to provide a structure that uses images and language to impart a meaning to retail products. Judith Williamson suggests that whereas an advertiser's main goal is to sell the products, good advertising requires the marketers to take into account the inherent qualities of the products as well as generate a meaning to the consumer. Williamson believes that advertisements sell more than just the consumer goods in the ads. The connections between the consumer and product are made by providing a *structure*, *method*, and *function* for using a product.[16] These connections generate associations of identity and status in consumer culture.

Context, Consumers, and Meaning

In 1997, Jean A. Hamilton's article "The Macro-Micro Interface in the Construction of Individual Fashion Forms and Meaning" addressed the transfer of individual fashion forms and their meanings from the *macro* (global) interface to the *micro* (individual) level. Her study delved into how culture and fashion arbiters globally influence consumers' interpretations of ideas associated with fashion goods and branding. Hamilton touched on issues of how and why merchandise is made and distributed. Hamilton's innovative argument focused on the use of storytelling to create the brand concept of continual consumption.[17] Hamilton's theoretical ideology suggested that through storytelling, a context is created to entice consumers to repurchase mass-produced items.

Hamilton's primary goal was to develop a model based on the notion that macro arbiters influence the micro-level meanings that consumers associate with their personal products. Her theoretical framework illustrated the movement from micro negotiations with the self → to negotiations with others → to fashion system arbiters → to cultural system arbiters (MACRO).[18] The following list includes the cultural and fashion system arbiters (macro) that underlie this process:

- Designers, product developers, and state planners in controlled economies
- Fashion forms and ideas created by designers and product developers
- The serendipitous (nonconspiratorial) interaction of the components on the delivery side (nonconsuming side) of the fashion systems; for example, designers, media, producers

(including manufacturers), distribution (including retailers)
- The conspiratorial interaction of components in the fashion system; major events/phenomena in the cultural system that influence fashion system participants and institutions as well as individual consumers; for example, war, national elections, political revolution, economic recession/depression
- Trends in the cultural system (or in subcultural systems) that may influence all or some participants in the fashion system or some individual fashion consumers; for example, Eastern religions, avant-garde music, art, films, literature
- Any or all of the above in combination with one another[19]

Hamilton recognized the ambivalence of fashion in the postmodern consumerist society, but her article emphasized the importance of decisions made by the cultural and fashion system arbiters. These decisions serve as persuasive devices for consumers. Because fashion garments carry no meanings and are signifiers only of themselves, it is the arbiters who give them meaning through selling context and/or display. Moreover, the arbiters must always be aware of what will appeal to a particular consumer or niche of the market; failure to do so could result in a loss in sales.

As Hamilton notes, the QVC television network connects meaning to consumer goods by displaying items and creating "selling stories" about the products' function and aesthetics. The consumer listens to the story and begins to relate to the item. The item begins to have a meaning associated with it, and the consumer feels the need to add it to his or her collection. This collection of goods serves to establish an individual's identity.[20]

An example of how fashion system arbiters create contextual meaning for products is found in the Joan Rivers line of jewelry that is promoted on QVC. Joan Rivers and QVC are the fashion arbiters of her jewelry collection. QVC has a database of information about previous customers who have purchased Rivers's jewelry. The company also knows what previous scripted segments of its show sold the most jewelry. Therefore, when Rivers is on QVC discussing her jewelry line, she may discuss the product referring to topics and the characteristics of her market niche. Also, when she is on the air, Rivers listens and talks to callers who have previously bought her jewelry. These callers tell Rivers about their experiences with the jewelry and how they wear it. The viewer who is watching may relate to Rivers, her jewelry, or the stories, as well as discussions she has had with the callers and other QVC employees on the air. The jewelry becomes signified through the selling context that is created around it. Without the context, the jewelry is less enticing for consumption.

In his article "Texture and Taboo: The Tyranny of Texture and Ease in the J. Crew Catalog," Matthew DeBord discusses the relevance of J.Crew's reinvention of mail-order catalogue sales in the postmodern era. By creating retail catalogues that depict hyperreal lifestyles, J.Crew purposefully entices consumers to purchase basic products that they probably already own. According to DeBord, the catalogue became a work of art that creates an aura of exclusiveness and allows consumers to shop from the privacy of their own homes. The catalogue has created lifestyles that are fantasized and almost surreal.[21]

Since DeBord's 1997 study, the J.Crew catalogue has continued to present models in fantasy settings, creating a visually perceived relaxed attitude. What is significant about DeBord's contextual analysis is his ability to recognize a retailer's talent to create meanings and fantasy associated with mass apparel for selling to consumers.

DeBord takes an art critic's view when discussing J.Crew's contextual marketing techniques. He makes no qualms about his frustration with J.Crew's manipulation of what he believes are disappointing and insignificant fashions.[22] Moreover, he does not admire the company's ability to generate revenue by creating total fantasy lifestyle advertising. Although DeBord takes a negative view of J.Crew's tactics, they do have redeeming qualities. The clothing marketed in J.Crew's catalogue reflects mass fashion at its most practical. Reasonable prices and the classic styling and versatility of the garments mean that they can virtually be worn until they wear out. The advertising strategy and lifestyle stories within J.Crew's catalogue reflect postmodern culture. The company attaches meaning to its products through the branding technique of storytelling.

Storytelling, Cultural Branding, and Emotions

Teri Agins reveals in her book, *The End of Fashion*, that the survival of designers and retailers is dependent on their proficiency in branding their products. Fashion, according to Agins, is not about products, but rather about how they are marketed and sold as a "brand image," or what she calls *lifestyle merchandising*. Whereas garments such as T-shirts, khaki pants, and jeans are staples found in many people's closets, what makes them unique or special is the meaning given to them through marketing campaigns.[23] This phenomenon suggests that although clothing is an essential component of popular culture, the actual garment itself has become secondary to the branding techniques used to sell it.

Lifestyle merchandising has been developed by designers such as Ralph Lauren, Tommy Hilfiger, Donna Karan, and Calvin Klein. While Lauren was repackaging the polo shirt, Hilfiger was reinventing the oxford shirt and Karan was creating new women's apparel; but it was Calvin Klein who re-branded denim jeans. He may well be the man you can blame for paying high prices for jeans today, such as True Religion and Diesel. Klein's 1980 advertising campaign featuring 15-year-old Brooke Shields stole the show (Figure 2.10). Long before the risqué advertising of Abercrombie & Fitch, it was this picture that launched a thousand words. Shields became embroiled in a major controversy. More importantly, consumers responded to this ad and began scavenging through major department stores in search of Calvin Klein *designer* jeans. The designer jeans craze was launched, and Calvin Klein had branded himself and his name as the king of denim jeans. He had created mass hysteria over denim and generated emotional responses in consumers across the nation.

In *Emotional Branding*, Mark Gobe points out that successful fashion brands are those that can capture the emotions and personal convictions of their customers. Gobe states, "Corporations clearly need to fine tune their focus on the consumer psyche and understand the importance of the constantly evolving trends in their consumers' lifestyles."[24] Gobe believes that it will be the norm for retailers to brand according to the needs of their spe-

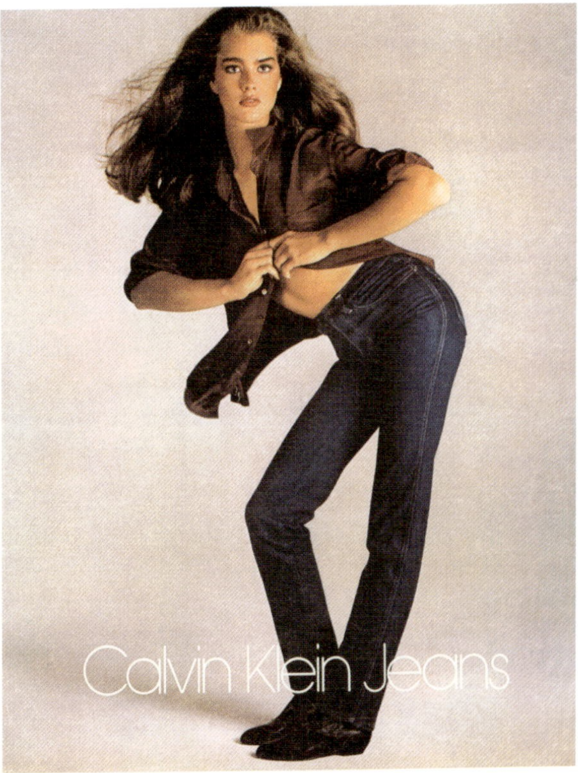

FIGURE 2.10 Calvin Klein Jeans 1980 advertisement featuring Brooke Shields.

cific target markets; companies that make emotional ties to consumers will rise to the top, whereas those who do not will fail.

Branding and Meaning Management

Another researcher who has continually focused on the meanings related to fashion branding is Grant McCracken. His research emphasizes that studying clothing is essential to understanding the cultural evolution of society. According to McCracken, meaning moves from the "culturally constituted world" to the gatekeepers of consumer goods to the individual consumer, all three add meaning to a brand as it passes through their domains. McCracken's theoretical models suggest that through social interaction, individuals (and eventually society) assign status to fashion-branded garments as well as types of consumer goods.[25]

In *Culture and Consumption II,* McCracken's research connects meaning to brand management. He emphasizes the need for brands to be studied from a meaning-based model instead of the traditional information-based model because of theoretical insufficiencies. For the development of the consumer market, meaning will become more effective in determining consumer patterns of consumption. According to McCracken, fashion marketing is one key to the creation and generation of future consumer consumption.[26]

McCracken suggests that context creates meaning for the product or service. He identifies nine different types of meanings that are usually targeted by companies: gender, lifestyle, decade, age, class and status, occupation, time and place, value, and fad, fashion, and trend meanings.[27] For McCracken, these meanings are determined by the company, its competitors and collaborators, customers, marketing segmentation, product and service positioning, market mix, and price of each consumer item.[28] He suggests that future scholars should study the various types of meanings used to create context around consumer goods. By examining all aspects of a company, consumers can start to see how the fashion branding story reflects products and services.

Fashion branding strategy is present in all aspects of consumption, from the store image to the advertising. For example, Abercrombie & Fitch (Figure 2.11), which encompasses the brands abercrombie, Hollister Co., RUEHL No.925, Gilly Hicks, as well as Abercrombie & Fitch, attempts to give each of its brands a unique identity. Why did Hollister choose to use a California beach house as the model for its stores? Does it truly reflect a brand image unique from the other divisions? How are the lifestyles that are represented by each of Abercrombie's divisions different? And if you look at each of its websites, are the product lines *really* that different if the meaning and story created by branding are removed?

Understanding the Research

The work of these researchers in the area of fashion branding can be combined to conclude that meaning, associations, emotions, and storytelling are the key ingredients for building fashion branding success. Jean Hamilton and Matthew DeBord revealed that consumer "relationships" to products are crucial for success in the marketplace. Hamilton examined "fashion and cultural

FIGURE 2.11 Hollister storefront in Columbus, Ohio mimics the exterior of a beach house.

arbiters" and celebrity endorsement on QVC, and DeBord demonstrated how stories are created to build attachments to simple products, such as khakis, polo shirts, and T-shirts. Stories created by branding executives and professionals utilize themes and symbols from contemporary culture, so that many individuals can understand and relate to them. Teri Agins has noted that lifestyle merchandising allows products to gain market share, and Marc Gobe revealed how important it is for "cultural stories" to make a connection to each consumer. Without an emotional attachment, a fashion brand is meaningless. Meaning-based understanding is essential when examining brands. Historically, branders were more interested in quantitative sales, but today's branding strategist is focused on targeting the consumer market by looking at people as individuals.

Conclusion

Fashion branding is a mixture of many elements and strategies that are generated to create product identity. This book provides a detailed look at the evolution of fashion companies that have managed to maintain a clear brand message. For example, compare the Burberry ad from the 1930s (see Figure 2.3) with a recent ad (Figure 2.12). What has happened to this brand? Has it evolved? What are the two different stories presented in these ads? What does the company's website look like? Where are its products sold? What do the sales associates look like in their stores? Does Burberry have commercials on television? What are the various types of products it is selling? Answering these questions for Burberry in particular and other fashion companies found in this book lead to a better understanding of the stories conveyed through fashion branding. An appreciation of fashion branding is essential if one is to become an analytical consumer and strategist, rather than just an observer.

FIGURE 2.12 A Burberry advertisement from 2008 reflects modern style, but calls attention to the company's longevity with "Established 1856."

Discussion Questions

1. How has fashion advertising changed since the mid-twentieth century? What are some of the differences between ads that appeared before the 1950s and those from the 1950s, 1960s, and today?
2. What are some of the theories related to fashion branding (i.e., Barthes and Baurdillard)? What do they say about fashion branding as a means of communicating with consumers? How do the contemporary ideas of Hamilton, DeBord, Agins, Gobe, and McCracken relate to those of Barthes and Baurdrillard?
3. What types of meanings does Grant McCracken associate with fashion products? Do you agree or disagree? If you disagree, what would you add to or delete from his list? Give an example of one of the meanings.

Exercise

Trace the history of the fashion brand Burberry. Examine its ads today and those from past campaigns. What are the differences? Has the target market changed? Did this fashion company follow its target market clients as they aged? Back up your research with clear examples.

RALPH LAUREN

CHAPTER THREE

THE HISTORY OF A KING

RALPH LAUREN

Lifestyle Merchandising

When considering *lifestyle merchandising,*[1] the name Ralph Lauren stands out. He has taken functional military garments, such as cargo pants and duffle coats, and traditional work clothes, such as canvas barn jackets and blue jeans, and turned them into luxury garments that sell for hundreds of dollars. Lauren's method is known as lifestyle marketing and association; he places practical garments in a luxury context. The luxury brand image leads consumers to associate Ralph Lauren products with high-end status. From a single concept for selling ties to the 2004 launch of a youth culture-inspired store called Rugby, Ralph Lauren has displayed a brand image that is "aspirational and classically iconic with an attitude uniquely its own"[2] for baby boomers as well as generations X, Y, and now Z.

Ralph Lauren has dedicated 40 years of his life to the creation of his brand image. The Ralph Lauren Polo line is featured on fashion runways and in every department store across the nation. However, contrary to popular belief, Ralph Lauren is not a traditional designer; he is a merchandiser. Lauren is the conceptual genius behind his brand, not the person who drafts patterns, sews strips of fabric, or sits behind the computer-aided design (CAD) software program. As the king of merchandising, he has total creative license to dream up ideas that influence his brand. His biography is a component of his brand; without Lauren, the man, the garments are worthless. Lauren has maintained control over every aspect of his business so that it perfectly reflects his vision.

There have been many articles and books written about Ralph Lauren. Recently, he published an autobiography about his ascent to the top of his field.[3] *Ralph Lauren* presents a glamorous life and highlights all of Lauren's wonderful accomplishments. Some biographies, such as *Genuine Authentic* by Michael Gross, are not always so complimentary,[4] whereas others, such as *Ralph Lauren: The Man, the Vision, the Style* by Colin McDowell, make him out to be a hero; a man among men.[5] However, the main purpose of this chapter is not to critique Ralph Lauren from a personal perspective, but to highlight his growth as a lifestyle merchandising branding powerhouse.

History of a Merchandiser

Ralph Lauren was born on October 14, 1939, the son of Russian Jewish immigrants. His real name was Ralph Lifshitz, but in his late teens, he and his brothers had their names changed to Lauren. Ralph Lauren had a normal childhood, with a modest up-

FIGURE 3.1 Ralph Lauren at his Spring 2007 collection show.

bringing. He grew up in the Bronx, New York, and lived with his parents in a two-bedroom apartment. He shared a room with his brothers throughout his childhood and often wore their hand-me-down clothes. He become accustomed to the worn look of the garments and eventually enjoyed the style of the apparel. Eventually, the casual look of Ralph Lauren line would reflect nostalgia for his childhood (see Figure 3.1).

Young Ralph purchased clothes from Army-Navy surplus stores, Alexander's discount store, and Discount of the Day.[6] Ralph enjoyed these clothes because he knew no one else would own them. According to most biographers, his personal appearance became an obsession. In his book, Michael Gross establishes the fact the Lauren is obsessed with his body, skin, and most obviously, his clothes.[7]

Although Lauren never finished college, he did attend City College for two years. His first position was at Brooks Brothers in the late 1950s. In the mid-1960s, Ralph Lauren took a position with a Boston-based tie manufacturer, Rivetz. Sources indicate that Lauren was an average salesman, but his appearance management was extraordinary.[8] He believed that by dressing in a particular style, he would be iconic in the manufacturing business. He utilized self-promotion as a way to stand above his peers and get attention from clients. Lauren's unique style allowed him to gain sales and a reputation. Whereas some thought his personal appearance was unusual, other viewed him as a genius. Ralph Lauren became skilled at networking in the New York garment industry. He learned early that building relationships was essential to creating his own brand.

In 1967, Beau Brummel, the Cincinnati-based tie firm, gave Ralph Lauren an opportunity to launch his own line of ties. By looking beyond the fashion trends at the time, Lauren's concept was to sell wider ties with a larger knot at the top. During a time when ties were only 2 to 3 inches wide, his ties measured 4 inches across.

The Polo Line

After attending a polo match and seeing the opulent lifestyle associated with the sport, Lauren put the cart in front of the horse, so to speak, and created the name of his product line—Polo—prior to any of the actual products. To Lauren, brand image was everything. Lauren also sold his ties at higher prices than the competition. To him, if the price was higher the client would perceive that quality was better. *Playboy* and the now defunct menswear periodical *Daily News Record* featured articles about Ralph Lauren's new ties. The title of the article in the *Record* was "The Big Knot."[9] This led to interest from buyers for Bloomingdale's and other high-end retailers. After his line of ties was established, from 1968 to 1969 Ralph Lauren expanded his Polo menswear line. Conceptualizing the perfect in-store presentation for his product, Lauren opened the first men's shop-within-a-shop for his collection (Figure 3.2) at Bloomingdale's in New York City.[10]

In 1971, Lauren established a line of tailored shirts for women, based on the cut of men's suits. That same year, he debuted the Ralph Lauren women's shop-within-a-shop at Bloomingdale's and introduced the Polo player logo on his product lines (Figure 3.3).[11] During that same year, Ralph Lauren opened his first store on Rodeo Drive in Beverly Hills, California. The store was financed by Jerry Magnin, whose great-grandfather started the luxury department store I. Magnin. This was quite an accom-

FIGURE 3.2 Interior of the Ralph Lauren menswear store in Chicago.

FIGURE 3.3 The Polo pony found on most Ralph Lauren sportwear.

plishment for the young merchant who had only been in the business for about five years. The store is also significant because it marked the very first freestanding store for an American designer brand. By 1980 there were seven more stores in the Ralph Lauren chain, in Fort Lauderdale, Atlanta, Houston, Detroit, Chicago, Palm Beach, and Dallas.[12]

The Polo logo shirt was introduced in 24 colors in 1972. The marketing campaign stated, "Every team has its color—Polo has 24."[13] Ralph Lauren hosted his first women's fashion show during this campaign. During this time, Ralph Lauren merchandise was sold in exclusive stores such as Bloomingdale's, Neiman Marcus, and Saks Fifth Avenue.[14]

Although the clothing line was hailed as extremely stylish, the fit of the garments was horrible. Ralph had used his wife Ricki Lauren and colleague Buffy Birrittella as the size models for the garments. Both were svelte, trim, and had very little cleavage; instead of using a standard-size size-8 model, Lauren has used women who were size 2. Because of this, most customers where unable to even fit their arms into the sleeves of the women's oxford shirts that Lauren marketed. These sizing issues were eventually remedied.[15]

Lauren continued to create menswear, women's wear, and accessories over the next several years. Then his brand's exposure was increased through a motion picture.

Films and Fragrance

In 1974, Ralph Lauren's design style was recognized around the world through the release of *The Great Gatsby*, starring Robert Redford and Mia Farrow. Although most of the garments for the movie were actually styled and constructed by costume designer Theoni V. Aldredge, Lauren inspired the men's garments. Aldredge won the Oscar for the costumes and was even asked to sell her fashion designs from the movies at the Bloomingdale's store in New York.

In 1976, Lauren received his second Coty Award for women's wear, and was inducted into the Coty Hall of Fame for menswear.[16] By this time, Ralph Lauren had established himself as a key figure in American design. Additionally, to grow his business in 1976, Lauren launched his Polo line for boys in major department stores. The line reflected his menswear, complete with ties, blazers, khakis, and oxford shirts bearing the embroidered polo player (Figure 3.4).

In 1977, with the assistance of costume designer Ruth Morley, Ralph Lauren received honorable mention in another motion pic-

FIGURE 3.4 Ralph Lauren advertisement from the 1990s. Note the young boy who is dressed to emulate the adults.

FIGURE 3.5 Polo advertisement featuring Ralph Lauren (*left*).

ture by providing the clothes for Diane Keaton and Woody Allen in the movie *Annie Hall*. With the launch of this film, a trend for eclectic combinations such as classics with vintage style became popular in men's and women's clothing. For the film, both Woody Allen and Diane Keaton wore Lauren's current fashion line.[17]

In 1978, Ralph Lauren launched a line inspired by the American West. Colin McDowell states, it "hailed (Lauren) as the man who 'recaptured' America for America and it rebuffs the erroneous impression that Ralph Lauren's fashion is too British."[18] With the launch of the Western product line, Lauren decided to actually become part of his brand image by posing in the ads (Figure 3.5). By modeling his own products, Lauren began to create the image that he was authentically Western. Even though he had never been a real cowboy, Lauren began to create the reality that surrounded his childhood fantasies of cowboys living on ranches. During this year Ralph Lauren also launched his first fragrances, Lauren for women and Polo for men. It was the first time ever that a design company introduced fragrances for both genders simultaneously.[19]

These two fragrances enabled Lauren to enter a new niche market of consumers who perhaps were avid fragrance and grooming purchasers, but not necessarily familiar with Lauren's clothing line. The distinct Polo scent of leather, wood, tobacco, basil, and oakmoss makes it immediately identifiable. The floral (violet, carnation, rose) and wood spice of Lauren for women is also quite distinct. These two fragrances are still quite popular. The company even created an 8-ounce spray bottle (which is very uncommon) of Polo, for those who are obsessed with the fragrance.

Refreshing the Image and Going Worldwide

In 1979, Lauren redefined his image with a unique 20-page marketing campaign using photographs by fashion photographer Bruce Weber in national magazines. As described by McDowell, "The ads featured little or no text, frequently using nonmodels, in which the clothes are seen as part of an overall lifestyle. The results, almost cinematic in breadth, captured the public imagination and have been frequently copied."[20]

The ads firmly established Lauren as a lifestyle brand. The popularity of the Weber photographs was instrumental to Ralph Lauren's ascent to international fashion mogul. With captions such as "Rough wear—it was made to be worn," the ad campaign was the model for today's lifestyle brand advertising. These ads inspired companies such as Abercrombie & Fitch, which also used Weber photographs to create its lifestyle advertising campaigns.

In 1981 Lauren debuted his Santa Fe collection, which influenced his designs throughout that decade (Figure 3.6). The collection was recognized by the international community as a substantial contribution to the world of fashion because it was the first to introduce the theme of the American West to high-end fashion. Ralph Lauren became known as the company that created the authentic spirit of America by using fashions that were inspired by the Western frontier. This fashion line continues to be significant in the United States and Europe. The Santa Fe collection generated an upscale image of Ralph Lauren as a lifestyle brand that presented a particular image of Americans to the international markets. The Santa Fe collection romanticized the American West, establishing an image of American fashion with cowboy boots and hats, western shirts, denim jeans, big-buckled belts, rawhide fringe jackets, prairie skirts, flannel shirts, and thermal henleys.

The Westernwear frenzy crossed the ocean in 1981 with the opening of a Polo shop on Bond Street in London. The store was an instant success. Ralph Lauren was the first American design company to have its own European boutique.

Home Goods, Out of Africa, and More Fragrances

Lauren then turned his attention to products for the home[21] to expand his merchandising empire. The venture would extend the Lauren lifestyle into the consumer's home environment. The ads for the three home design lines—Log Cabin, Thoroughbred, and New England—displayed images of traditional home fur-

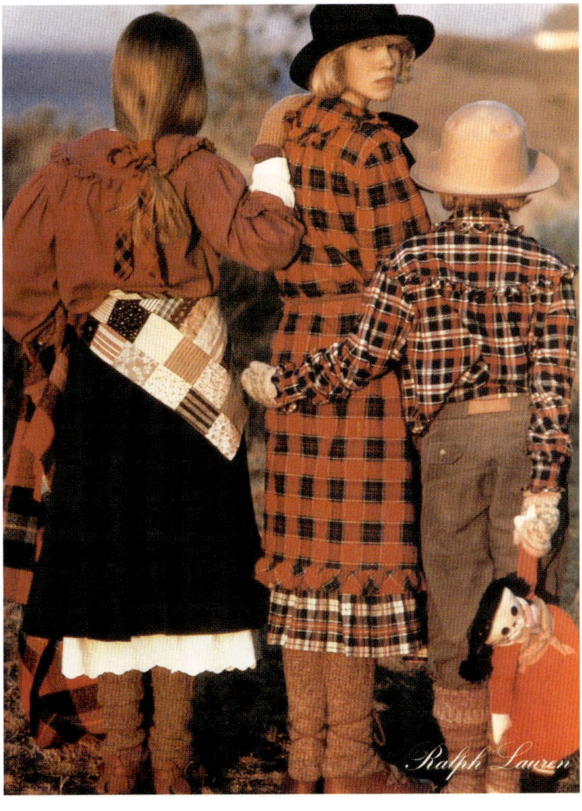

FIGURE 3.6 Advertisement for Ralph Lauren's Santa Fe collection.

nishings with a rugged twist, and simply stated "How Tradition Begins." Each line had its own branded message. Log Cabin reflected a luxury cowboy suite and Thoroughbred was reflective of an English country house.[22]

Ralph Lauren's 1984 designs were very likely influenced by the movie *Out of Africa,* which starred Meryl Streep and Robert Redford. Lauren had remained friends with Redford since *The Great Gatsby. Out of Africa* was in preproduction when Lauren released his 1984 line, which featured traditional Safari styles with the rugged and worn style that is now immediately identifiable as Ralph Lauren. Many of Lauren's ads during the time looked as if they were mimicking stills from the movie.

In 1986, Ralph Lauren opened his flagship store in New York City, in a building that was previously a mansion belonging to the Rhinelander family. The building, located on Madison Avenue at 72nd Street, was completely renovated. This store was to become a Ralph Lauren masterpiece. The flagship store reflected everything the Ralph Lauren brand stood for in the mind of the consumer (Figure 3.7). The first Ralph Lauren boutique in Paris also opened that year.

The Empire Grows

Lauren's company continued to flourish, launching new product lines, expanding into the international market, creating award-winning fragrances, and sharing the wealth through philanthropic efforts. Ralph Lauren's success is the result of networking, creative thinking, increasing public awareness, strategy, and, most importantly, a focus on a clear vision for the brand—a consistent image and story.

From Safari to Rugby

The Lauren image of high quality and luxury extends to the award-winning fragrances. Safari for men and women was

FIGURE 3.7 The Ralph Lauren flagship store on Madison Avenue and 72nd Street in New York City.

launched in 1990. It was the first lifestyle fragrance that was merchandised with a range of accessories and home furnishings to complement it. The Safari fragrance won the coveted Fragrance Foundation's FiFi award for Fragrance Star of the Year in 1990 and again in 1991. The Romance fragrance (for women) was launched in 1998 and received the FiFi Fragrance Star of the Year and best national advertising campaign awards. Romance for Men soon followed and received both awards in 1999.

In fashion, the Polo Sport line was launched in 1993 with a store at 888 Madison Avenue, across the street from the Rhinelander store. The Polo Sport brand marked a change in the advertising style of Ralph Lauren, as well as a shift in the target market for the company. It was during this campaign that Jamaican model Tyson Beckford became the leading model for

Ralph Lauren. Prior to the launch of Polo Sport, Lauren had used primarily Caucasian models in his ad campaigns. Beckford's face would be the new look of Ralph Lauren over the next few years, appearing in ads for the fragrance Polo Sport, for underwear (Figure 3.8), and eventually for the Purple Label division.

By using Beckford in his ads, Lauren made a strong statement and stretched his concept of lifestyle merchandising to a new ethnic market. At the time, rappers, hip-hop artists, and other African American celebrities were wearing baggy clothes. MTV and VH-1 played videos of these stars and their baggy street clothes with underwear waistbands exposed. The look started to influence street fashions. Lauren recognized that this market had big spending power. Beckford's face and the ads for Polo

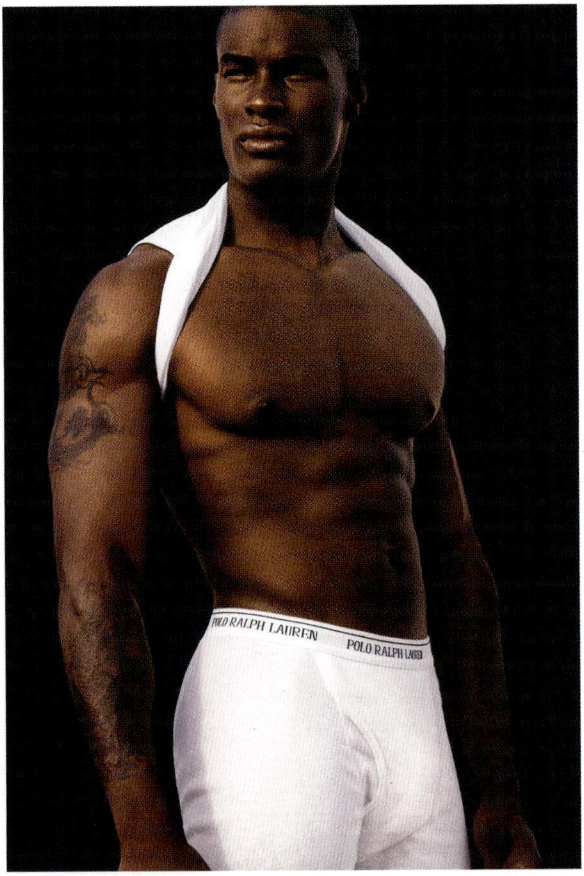

FIGURE 3.8 Polo Ralph Lauren men's underwear ad featuring Tyson Beckford.

Ralph Lauren underwear would connect the brand with this ethnic street market, leading to an increase in sales of underwear as well as other Polo Sport items. This line was less expensive than other Lauren products and was cut, designed, and fitted in a baggy silhouette reflective of rappers and hip-hop artists.

Lauren also introduced the RRL line in 1993, which was named after his Colorado ranch. The RRL products reflected a romanticized life of a cowboy, as seen on the classic television show *Bonanza*. Flannel shirts, denim jeans, and belts all carried a hefty price and looked as if they had been worn for years (think very high-end grunge with cowboy hats, boots, and spurs). This look was one of Lauren's favorites, with form-fitting cut that reflected Ralph Lauren's personal style.

The Lauren Purple Label, which debuted in 1994, is a line of men's tailored clothing. This advertising campaign also featured Ralph Lauren as a model. The clothing was made from finer fabrics with tailored silhouettes. The line was introduced when casual Fridays became all the rage in the business sector. This line was designed to bring custom-made garments to the retail sector.[23]

Lauren added paints to his home goods' line in 1995. By adding paint, he continued the lifestyle branding messages his company had built over the years. The colors ranged from Gray Flannel, Suede, and River Rock to Duchesse Satin.[24] The paints added a finishing touch to complete the look of his home furnishings brands.

In 1996, Polo Sport Women was introduced and won the FiFi Award for Best National Advertising Campaign. Also, Polo Jeans Co., a line of casual wear for the young, was launched. That same year, Lauren by Ralph Lauren was released. This moderately priced women's collection was reminiscent of the traditionally tailored Polo-style line that Lauren had done in the early 1970s. This division of the Polo brand became Lauren's better women's sportswear line found in all major department stores.[25]

Polo Sport launched the RLX line of authentic high-tech sports clothing in 1997 and opened the Ralph Lauren restaurant adjacent to the Chicago flagship store in 1999. That same year, Polo Ralph Lauren acquired Canadian specialty retailer Club Monaco.[26] Known for their sleek and narrow fashion assortment in basic colors, Club Monaco continues to operate locations in the United States and Canada.

RalphLauren.com was launched in 2000, allowing consumers to buy merchandise on the Web. Eventually the Create Your Own Polo feature was added to the website, as well as an online magazine, called *RL Magazine*. During the 2002–2003 fashion season, Lauren creations were shown on the runways in Milan; the Purple Label line for men was shown in the spring along with a women's version; Blue Label, and the company's first children's-only store opened on Madison Avenue. It was the first freestanding children's wear store, featuring the same quality and style of his adult Polo line (Figure 3.9).

Ralph Lauren's division dedicated to Generation Y—Rugby—was launched in 2004. The Rugby line represents a nostalgic look at the Ivy League experience and the ideals of a collegiate setting. The store's focus of a preppy look with a twist is understood by the shopper who visits the store. Traditionally, whereas icons such as whales, alligators, and ducks are embroidered on preppy garments, Lauren uses a skull-and-crossbones for the Rugby product line. Some brand associates wear dreadlocks, colored hair, tattoos, and even body piercings, unlike the crispy clean look of those at retailers such as Abercrombie & Fitch or American Eagle, who target the same market.

Some critics have stated that this store is Ralph Lauren's response to the popularity of Abercrombie & Fitch. However, this author disagrees. The product assortment in the Rugby stores is more European than that found at Abercrombie & Fitch and the ambiance of the store is completely different. Where Abercrombie uses darkness, fragrance, and loud music to attract customers, Rugby uses light, custom design, and DJs that play music at specific times. It creates a more personal approach.

Lauren continues to spread the word around the world. In 2007, Lauren opened a flagship store in Moscow.

A Design Star Is Born

The standard of excellence associated with Lauren and his company has been recognized repeatedly. In 1992, Ralph Lauren received the Council of Fashion Designers of America (CFDA) Lifetime Achievement Award, one of four top honors he has received from the organization over the years. In 1997 Polo Ralph Lauren became a publicly traded company on the New York Stock Exchange, and in 2001 Ralph Lauren was inducted into first Fashion Walk of Fame in New York.

Lauren's philanthropic endeavors are well known. In 1993 Polo Sport fragrance sponsored the first annual Race to Deliver.

FIGURE 3.9 Ralph Lauren children's wear advertisement.

This event raised funds for the charitable organization God's Love We Deliver, which provides hot meals for housebound people with AIDS/HIV.[27] Lauren's support for breast cancer campaigns was rewarded with the first Humanitarian Award from the Nina Hyde Center for Breast Cancer,[28] which was presented to Lauren by Diana, Princess of Wales. In 2000 RalphLauren.com donated $6 million to establish The Ralph Lauren Center for Cancer Care and Prevention at North General Hospital in Harlem, and the Pink Pony campaign donates 10 percent of the proceeds from that line to cancer research and awareness programs.

Lauren's commitment to the arts and education was recognized by Brandeis University with an honorary doctorate of letters. In 1998 a corporate gift of $13 million from Ralph Lauren went to the Save America's Treasures Campaign to help preserve the flag that inspired Francis Scott Key's "The Star Spangled Banner." In the wake of the World Trade Center attack on September 11, 2001,[29] Lauren established the American Heroes Fund, raising $4 million for the relief effort and a scholarship fund for the children of victims. He continued his community relations with a $110,000 donation to the Abyssinian Church of Harlem. The church thanked Ralph Lauren with an award given by *Vogue* magazine's Andre Leon Talley who stated:

> What Michelangelo was to the Sistine chapel, what Carl Sandberg was to the American iambic pentameter, and what F. Scott Fitzgerald was to the grammar of the American romance story, Ralph Lauren is to American Style. His vision, his commitment to excellence, his incredible style and grace, his elegance, and his profound philanthropic spirit speaks volumes for this great leader and man.[30]

Today, the Ralph Lauren Foundation continues to support a number of charities.

The Lauren brand is associated with a healthy, active lifestyle, and the company has sponsored a number of sporting events. Polo Sport RLX sponsored the U.S. World Cup mountain bike team in 1997, and Polo was the official fashion sponsor of the 2006 Wimbledon championships, designing sweaters, shorts, pants, and belts for the tennis players. In 2008 Lauren was named an official outfitter of the 2008 U.S. Olympic and Paralympic teams, designing the outfits for the opening and closing ceremonies as well as some street clothes for the athletes to wear while in Beijing.

Discussion Questions

1. Is Ralph Lauren a designer? Why or why not?
2. Where did Ralph Lauren work prior to working for himself? Why do you think this experience was beneficial to his career?
3. Currently, how many divisions does Ralph Lauren operate under his name? Can you identify the target market of each division? Are they homogenous or diverse?
4. What is your favorite division of Ralph Lauren? How does that division emulate your personal lifestyle?
5. How has Ralph Lauren built on his original brand to create an empire and an almost unparalleled career in fashion? Can you think of someone else who compares to him?

Exercise

Most designers and merchandisers that have an established name have been working for a while in the retailing, manufacturing, or design industry. Identify someone who you feel reflects the type of fashion brand you would develop and write a 750 word essay on his or her career. How has each of that person's experiences helped them develop a successful brand? What do you think the future of their brand will be?

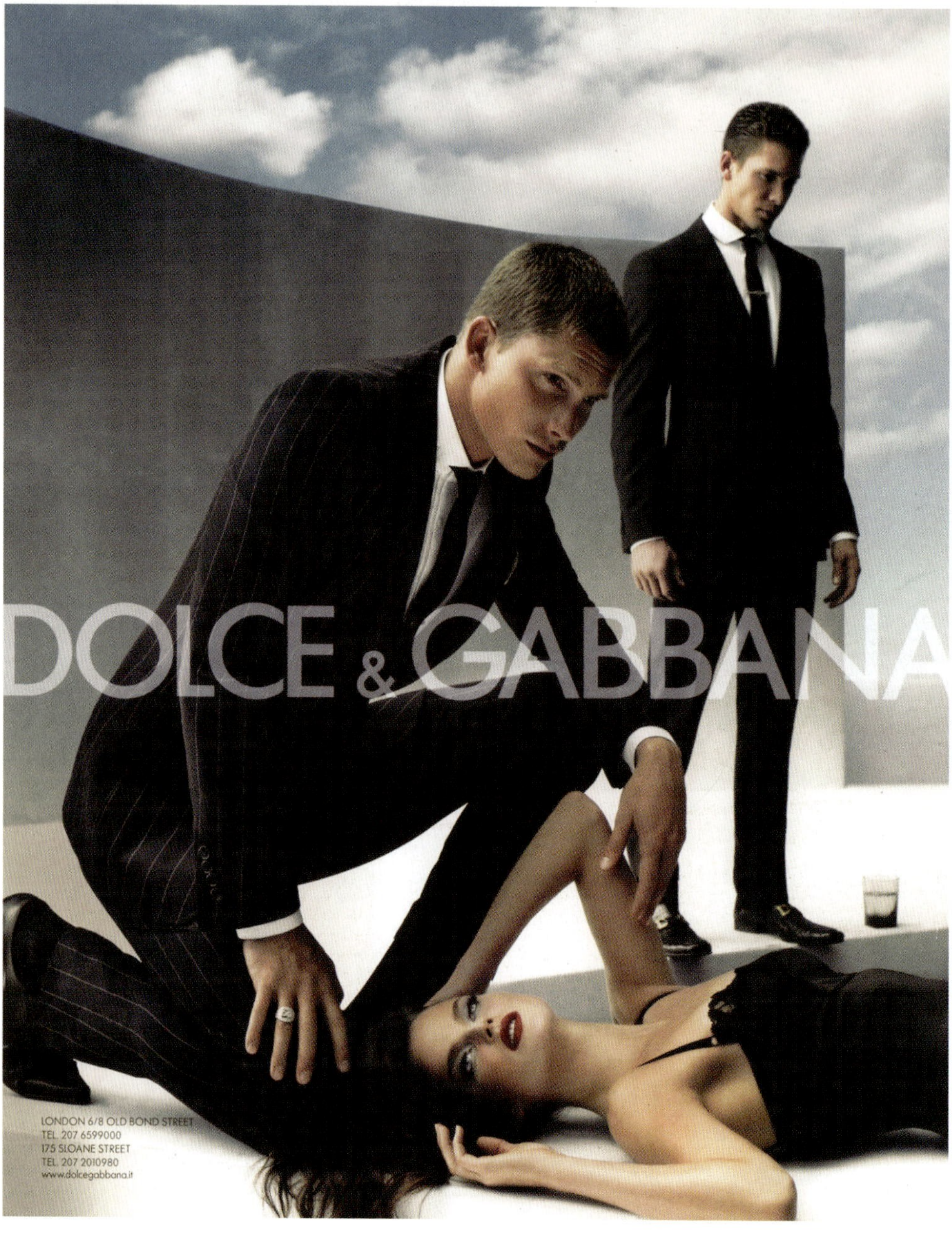
DOLCE & GABBANA
LONDON 6/8 OLD BOND STREET
TEL. 207 6599000
175 SLOANE STREET
TEL. 207 2010980
www.dolcegabbana.it

CHAPTER FOUR

MASS LUXURY STYLE

DOLCE & GABBANA

Fantastically Sexy!!!

If Cinderella ever needed to replace her fairy godmother, she would call Dolce & Gabbana. This design team creates products that sparkle and has managed to change the staunch and uptight image of luxury fashion, making it fun and exciting for everyone. No longer is upscale fashion just for the stereotypical uptight high-end customer; it is now for a new type of customer. The branding stories of Dolce & Gabbana have targeted those who may not normally be expected to enjoy high-quality fashions—the avant garde, bohemian, ethnically diverse, eccentric, unique, nontraditional, and unusual have been part of this design duo's success. They have embraced everyone. Dolce & Gabbana's branding story is about taking the nontraditional fashion consumer and demonstrating how they can be stylish and sophisticated in their own way. The branding story of Dolce & Gabbana stems from the pair's own lifestyle and views of the world. This brand story reflects diversity!

The Dolce & Gabbana Story

Domenico Dolce was born on September 13, 1958, in the Sicilian village of Polizzi and his partner, Stefano Gabbana, was born on

November 14, 1962, in Milan. They met in 1980 while working for the same design company and instantly had chemistry—for fashion and each other.[1] For many years, Stefano Gabbana and Domenico Dolce were partners in both business and life. By literally spending day and night together, they were able to build a multidivisional corporation over the course of 25 years. The two designers became role models in the world of luxury designer fashion and to many gay and lesbian fans, who bought their products because of quality and in reaction to their advertising campaigns. In 2005 the couple split up, but they continue as business partners.

The Dolce & Gabbana brand reflects a postmodern world composed of culture, traditions, and the designers' Mediterranean upbringing. This global brand is distinguishable from all others. Both designers understand Italian charm, how to maintain class while simultaneously entertaining consumers, and how to interpret mass street style into luxury fashion-branded apparel. They dress consumers of all ages—from baby boomers to generation Z—around the world.[2]

The Dolce & Gabbana group consists of three distinct brands: Dolce & Gabbana, D&G, and D&G Junior. The latter two are premium-priced product lines that are more accessible to mass consumers. Similar to Ralph Lauren, Dolce & Gabbana have become a full lifestyle brand. But whereas Ralph Lauren tends to cater to the more traditional consumer, Dolce & Gabbana is all about sparkle (commonly known as *bling*).

Groundbreaking Ads

Dolce & Gabbana's advertising campaigns have added to their controversial image. Borrowing from cultural and social ideologies as well as from current trends, each of the ads is a story that increases the brand's mysterious image. These ads represent life from a unique perspective, allowing the consumer to experience unique lifestyles, individuals, and even surreal dreamlike stories. They are almost cinematic. The viewer is expected to internalize the images in each branding story to create their own story. This supports the notion that brands must create stories and emotional attachments to consumers in order to sell products. Dolce & Gabbana are masters of this technique.

Stefano Gabbana and Domenico Dolce sometimes include themselves as models in their ad campaigns. For example, in February 2007, both appeared in a fashion spread in *W Magazine* (Figure 4.1) that reflected the true spirit of the brand. In Figure 4.1, the viewer sees Stefano Gabbana at home in his bedroom. In the picture he wears nothing but a pair of underwear (possibly

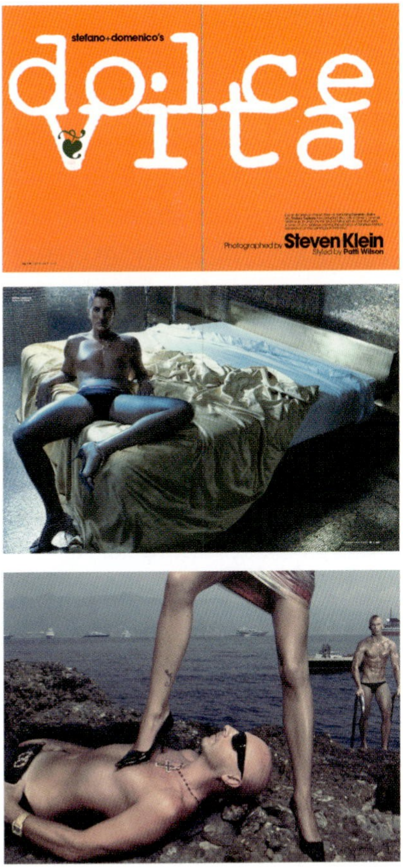

FIGURE 4.1 Stefano Gabbana photographed in his bedroom and Domenico Dolce (with sunglasses) photographed for *W Magazine* in 2007.

Dolce & Gabbana underwear) while creating what appears to be a satirical statement about his personal life. He allows the reader to see how he can easily be in touch with his feminine side by sporting a pair of spike-heeled open-toe beaded sandals. Traditional stereotypes have suggested that gay men dress as women, have the desire to be women, or are effeminate, but Stefano Gabbana does not seem to care. Clearly, this photo suggests that he is comfortable with himself and will wear whatever he wishes. It also demonstrates to his female customers that he will wear the same high-heeled shoes he designs for them. He may be trying to say that they are just plain sexy. Whatever the case may be, Gabbana either has a shoe fetish or firmly believes in his product.

The same can be said for Domenico Dolce in Figure 4.1. In this photo, he is seen resting on the rocks by the water wearing a Dolce & Gabbana bathing suit. He is dominated by a woman wearing spiked heels. She rests the spike of her heel firmly on his chest. However, he is comfortable and does not seem bothered by her assault. Because we (the viewers) know Dolce is gay, we know that he is not admiring what is under her dress. Maybe he is awaiting rescue from the ripped muscular blonde watching the assault, or he is simply making the statement that his female customers are in charge. He pretends to be their humble servant; he is there to make them beautiful.

Both ads reflect the freedom of the designers to live life their own way. They also reveal that Dolce & Gabbana are aware of the reputation and image of their brand. Both photos have bling, with Gabbana's gold-toned bedspread and walls and Dolce's gold accessories and what appears to be a golden-bronzed beach hunk. The ads exude sparkle, attitude, sex, storytelling, uniqueness, irony, sarcasm, self-confidence, luxury, and maybe a little shock value.

But there is a side of this design team that remains grounded. Although they are risqué, they are also nonthreatening because they are so comfortable with who they are and what they represent. In this chapter we explore the team's quintessential customer; how they won the hearts of the gay and lesbian community; how their line has expanded into items such as sunglasses, denim, children's clothes, fragrance, fine dining, and even books; and finally, how they continue to create advertising that masterfully reflects a luxury image.

Who Are D&G's Customers?

Dolce & Gabbana have surrounded themselves with high style, sparkle, and bling, but they love *real people* as opposed to the emaciated body types we have come to expect in luxury fashion. In their second fashion show in 1986, instead of real models, the team used friends that included: actors, artists, dancers, architects, and even university professors, to model their clothes.[3] They love hips, waists, curves, bustlines, and a woman with a little meat on her bones. Although Madonna, whose body type is far from typical, wore their clothes in her *Truth or Dare: In Bed with Madonna* documentary that made the designers famous in the United States, they are better known in Italy for dressing the voluptuous Sophia Loren and the iconic Anna Magnani. This team designs for Monica Bellucci, Isabella Rossellini, Kylie Minogue, and Angelina Jolie, among other celebrities. Additionally, Dolce & Gabbana prove their love of curvaceous real women by featuring them in their ads (Figure 4.2). Dolce & Gabbana believe that a woman should be strong, self-confident, and know that others like her, too. In their words:

> She is a cosmopolitan woman who has toured the world, but who doesn't forget her roots. A woman who indifferently wears extremely sexy bras that can be seen under sheer clothes, contrasting them with the very masculine pinstripe suits complete with tie and white shirt or a men's

> vest. She always wears very high heels which, in any case, give her both an extremely feminine and sexy way of walking and unmistakable posture. She loves that so-masculine cap imported from Sicily and the rosary of the first Communion that she wears as a necklace. She can indifferently be a manager, wife, mother, or lover, but she is always—and in whatever case—thoroughly a woman.[4]

Brooke Shields has appeared as one of D&G's celebrity endorsers. She is the ultimate D&G woman who has risen above adversity. She is cosmopolitan, sexy, risqué, and dynamic, as well as a career woman, wife, and mother.

Dolce & Gabbana believe their male target customer is a man who takes care with his appearance, is detail oriented, and definitely a leader. He is the man who looks great whether he is in office attire or jeans and a T-shirt. He is a man who makes the rules, but is not governed by them. He is charismatic and charming. He is free to be an individual, which is what makes him successful.[5]

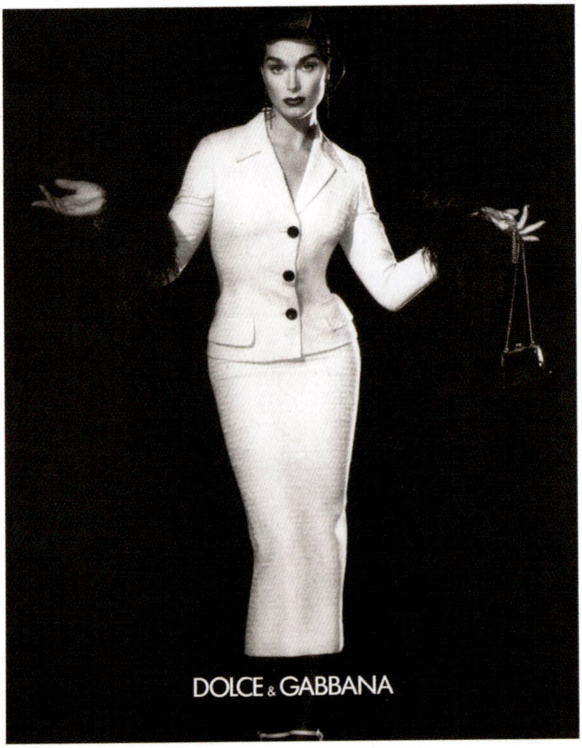

FIGURE 4.2 Brooke Shields for Dolce & Gabbana, 1995.

This element of individualism was used by Dolce & Gabbana in their 1994 advertising campaigns. To gain new customers for the licensed D&G division of their brand, Dolce & Gabbana launched a series of ads aimed at diverse target markets. This campaign featured "alternative" couples—punks, goths, multi-ethnic, gays, lesbians, and so on. Dolce & Gabbana was the first luxury brand to blatantly display the homosexual lifestyle. The gay and lesbian community viewed the ads as positive and uplifting (Figure 4.3),[6] and homosexuals supported the message by purchasing Dolce & Gabbana apparel. Unlike Versace and Abercrombie & Fitch, who *suggest* homoeroticism in some of their ads, D&G had no qualms about displaying the gay lifestyle. After all, it allowed the company's founders to *out* themselves to the public.

FIGURE 4.3 D&G was launched in 1994 featuring gay and lesbian lifestyles as shown in this ad. The new D&G brand became a huge success.

To many, the most shocking element of this advertising campaign was the context in which many of the couples were posed. Instead of being featured in luxury mansions, the campaign featured young couples in *real*, homelike contexts. Another key element was the young age of the models. By featuring younger couples, Dolce & Gabbana were making the statement that young gays and lesbians were comfortable with their lifestyles and were no longer hiding the fact that they were homosexuals. With these ads, homosexuality was being blatantly displayed in the luxury market across the globe! Mike Wilke of the Commercial Closet (an organization dedicated to the study of images of gays and lesbians in advertising) has noted that these ads put Dolce & Gabbana on the fashion map with the gay community. His organization holds the two designers in high honor because of their pioneering efforts.[7]

One might start to think that this would turn off many customers, or that those who were more traditional might not support the brand. But Dolce & Gabbana saw an increase in sales after the launch of this ad campaign.

INTERVIEW
How Does Fashion Branding Influence a Multiethnic Asian Male Consumer? Talking with Edward Choi Augustyn

Ralph Lauren demonstrates that fashion brands can be global. Most fashion brands, such as Lauren, are currently trying to reach ethnic markets, especially the male market. Currently, ads featuring ethnic men seem to focus on the black or Latino market (as seen with Ralph Lauren's Tyson Beckford). However, one target segment of males that has been neglected by fashion researchers is Asian men. This topic will become crucial as the Asian market grows and

this male customer becomes more focused on fashion. Retired performer and Asian American male fashionista Edward Choi Augustyn understands the critical nature of this business strategy and weighs in on the subject.

Please describe your ethnic mix, educational background, and professional experience.
My ethnic background is half Korean and half Caucasian. I was a professional ballet dancer for ten years before returning to college and graduate school (BA in Anthropology from Marlboro in Vermont and MFA in Dance from Mills in Oakland). I taught as a visiting assistant professor in dance for three years before deciding to pursue a career in nursing. I am now finishing prerequisite classes before starting the accelerated nursing BSN program at Drexel University in the fall of 2008.

Was it difficult to grow up as a multiethnic child?
In some sense it was because I lived in a primarily white, working-class neighborhood as a child. I was viewed as different and kids pick up on that right away. However, in Chicago, this was in the era of desegregation where the school system was actively promoting racial integration. Back in the 1980s, I attended Chicago's premiere magnet high school. One of its primary missions was volunteer integration through academic excellence and selective admissions. Middle-class African American kids were the majority with a healthy mix of white, Latino, and Asian teens. I loved the diversity!

How do you think being multiethnic has influenced your purchasing decisions and how you look at fashion brands?
At first I did not really think that this had bearing on my purchasing decisions, but as I grow older, I can see that my tastes for particular brands were highly influenced by my Asian her-

itage. Within the past five years one brand in particular caught my fancy, and that is Diesel. In my current collection two items really stand out to me and they both have an Asian flair. One item is a black polo that has a medium print of red and yellow dragons on both sides of the buttons and on the right back shoulder.

I also love a pair of gray cargos that, unlike many cargos, have pockets that are streamlined and do not poof out. I love the detailing on these pants. They have heavy buttons that look like pewter with red etchings. The pockets are lined with heavy black fabric and the waistband is reinforced with the black and red lining.

I also enjoy the anticollegiate look; in other words, I like dark, dirty colors with fits that drape but still outline shape. In summer, I really like wrinkled linen, cotton mixes in browns and greens. In some sense this reminds me a bit of my idea of Korean peasant clothing, or if you think of karate movies portraying ancient battle scenes where the action heroes are wearing loose tunic-style pants that you can move in.

Does the use of multiethnic models in fashion ads affect your fashion choices?

I love seeing multiethnic models, although I do not think they influence my purchasing decisions. I know that Diesel's ads and models do not influence me to shop there. I certainly take notice of these models. For example, Tyson Beckford and Naomi Campbell, although seen as prominent African American models, I believe, both have Asian blood in them. I am seeing a lot more Asian and Asian mixed male models these days. Look at the success of Kimora Lee Simmons and her show *Kimora: Life in the Fab Lane*; she is half Asian, too. I can't remember seeing this in my youth except for actor Richard Wong who was a former dancer turned actor.

The Growth of the Dolce & Gabbana Brand

Shortly after they met in 1980, Gabbana and Dolce began plans to establish themselves as a design team. By 1982, the couple had established a design consultancy in Milan. After finding wealthy financers to back their line in 1985, Dolce & Gabbana made a splash with a fashion show in their small studio space.[8] They then gained exposure at international runway shows, establishing a strong presence in the area of prêt-à-porter. The team has had a steady line of successes ever since.

In 1991, Dolce & Gabbana won their first award, the Woolmark award for the most innovative menswear collection. The ensuing years brought numerous accolades from various fashion organizations: Designer of the Year award for menswear from the reader's of Britain's *FHM Magazine* (1996 and 1997); Footwear Designer of the Year from *Footwear News* (1997); Style award from Russian *Harper's Bazaar* (1999)[9]; "T de Telva" award for the best international designers from Spanish magazine *Telva* (2000); Best Designer(s) of the Year for outstanding achievement *Gentleman's Quarterly* (2003); New York Fashion Group International award for outstanding achievement in Italian design (2003)[10]; Best International Designers, *British Elle* Style Awards (2004); and in September 2005, *Russian GQ* gave Gabbana and Dolce their Men of the Year Award for the year's best international designers.

Dolce & Gabbana decided to protect its lines against counterfeiting in 1997 and introduced an anti-imitation system. The goal of the system was to hinder duplication of their products, safeguarding its clientele as well as the merchandise. This system of anti-imitation principally consists of the use of safety holograms (showing an ampersand [&]), together with a series of micro-texts that reproduce the trademark.[11]

These graphics were designed and copyrighted by Dolce & Gabbana. The hologram is produced and guaranteed by the Italian State Printing Works and Mint. The anticounterfeiting letters used by the Dolce & Gabbana and D&G lines consist of a certificate of authenticity bearing the hologram. A woven label with a heat-impressed trademark and hologram is placed inside every garment. This safety seal contains an identification thread that is reactive to ultraviolet rays. A woven label with the Dolce & Gabbana logo incorporates the same identification thread. Furthermore, the company has stipulated agreements with customs authorities throughout the world with the intention of monitoring the articles bearing its trademark. So far this system has proven very successful for the team, which has substantially limited counterfeit goods in comparison to other luxury brands.[12] Dolce & Gabbana have attained global success in part through their attention to the details of their core business.

There are currently more than 80 Dolce & Gabbana boutiques around the globe and the company continues to reach new markets. For example, a new boutique was opened in Beverly Hills in May 2008 and others are planned in China (Shenyang and Dalian) and the Middle East; the latter represents over 5 percent of the company's total volume in sales. The concept for the new stores is reminiscent of the 1970s, with lustrous chrome and lush carpets. The decor as well as the products will epitomize the Dolce & Gabbana brand.[13] The company plans to open its largest Dolce & Gabbana boutique in Moscow, one of its largest markets,[14] in 2009. The brand is available in over 2,150 retail outlets around the world.

From Fragrances to Eateries

Through licensing agreements, the Dolce & Gabbana brand has extended into women's fragrance. In 1993 Dolce & Gabbana Pour Femme won the prestigious international prize from the Perfume Academy for the best feminine fragrance of the year. In 1995 Pour Homme was awarded prizes in three areas. The clean, fresh scent and the signature bottle wrapped in a blue velvet box was awarded the best new masculine fragrance of the year, the best packaging, and the best advertising by the Perfume Academy. In 1996, Pour Homme won another premiere award from France's so-called Oscar des Parfums.

The Dolce & Gabbana advertising campaigns are also highly regarded in the industry. The two designers gained recognition in Germany with the Leadaward in 2004 and again in 2006. This award is considered the most prominent prize for media, communication, and design in advertising. Advertising in these three categories must reflect a company's capability to convey strong brand images to the global market. Also in 2004, the company received the Interactive Key Award in Milan for the best website design for another licensed area—eyewear. In addition to design, the company received an award at the Bocconi University in Milan called the *Premio Risultati* for financial performance and best financial sales during the four-year period 1999 to 2002, and for its strategic branding and development.[15] In 2006, Dolce & Gabbana released the exclusive version of the RAZR cellular phone as a co-branding project with Motorola. The little phone grossed the company $30 million during the 2006-2007 sales year.

Current ventures for the design team include a new restaurant in Milan, called Gold. Like the rest of this team's brand image, the place sparkles! Sophia Banay, in an article for *Condé Nast Traveler*, noted that even the bathrooms of this restaurant are solid gold. She notes that the design team has left no stone unturned when it comes to the details in this restaurant.[16] Gold has expanded the brand to those who may not wear the clothes but want to experience the essence of Dolce & Gabbana.

During an interview with WWD.com, Dolce & Gabbana executive Cristiana Ruella stated that the company was expected to generate over $730.7 million in 2008. The sales of its current Spring 2008 collection rose 33 percent over the previous year's sales. Europe accounts for over 27 percent of the brand's sales with Japan at 17 percent, the rest of Asia at 14 percent, Italy at 12 percent, and the United States at 8 percent.[17] The executive team believes that by focusing on its original line, the growth of the company will continue. The strength of the brand has allowed the company to grow and to create many new avenues for global expansion.[18]

Everyone Deserves a Little Luxury—Reading the Ads

Dolce & Gabbana is a luxury brand that is distinguished by its ability to create satirical play and content in its fashions as well as its branding messages. This strong branding image has evolved over the years, but still remains faithful to its original standards—the integrity of the products, the image of unconventional luxury, continuous innovation, and the company's Italian origins.

In the twenty-first century this brand has diversified its marketing efforts to reflect style in simple things such as men's underwear, fragrance, and sunglasses (Figure 4.4). By mixing its couture with these everyday items, the company allows all people to indulge in what is perceived as luxury. Many people accept rather exorbitant prices (sunglasses, for example, retail between $350 and $400) because of the products' status appeal.

The ads create a context for simple items, such as sunglasses, that leads people to buy them based on the aesthetic of the brand message. For example, Figure 4.4 works on two levels. It is a simple representation of the product, but if the viewer "reads" the advertisement it becomes clear that Dolce & Gabbana has created a context for the product that reflects a particular style and culture. In this ad, the young woman (who happens to be the supermodel Coco Rocha) represents luxury style. The model is grasping a stringed musical instrument, which implies that she is a musician (i.e., an artist). This is reinforced when the model's identity is revealed because Coco Roca *is* an artist—an

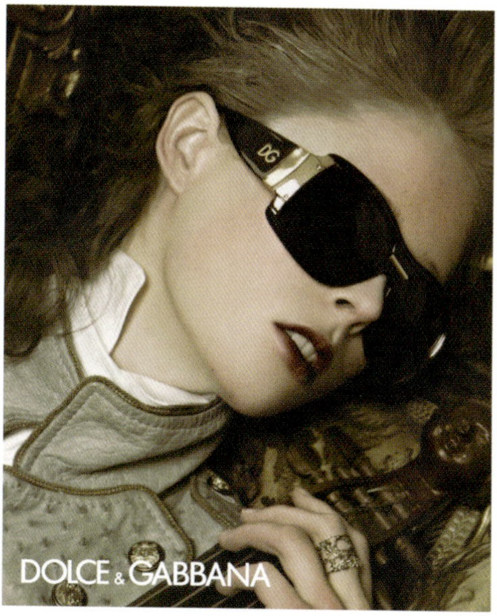

FIGURE 4.4 A 2006 advertisement for Dolce & Gabbana sunglasses, featuring Coco Rocha.

Irish dancer-turned-model. The gold ring and high-collared leather jacket embellished with gold buttons add to the sparkle and shine that is the essence of the Dolce & Gabbana fashion brand image.

D&G Junior and Menswear

The perception of luxury extends to Dolce & Gabbana's men's and children's lines as well. D&G Junior has led to the company's status as a global brand. The luxury and luster of style that is Dolce & Gabbana is clearly seen in this adolescent fashion line that features its own unique qualities (Figure 4.5). What is wonderful about this division of D&G is that the designers have created a line that is exclusively for kids without mimicking the style of adults. In other words, D&G Junior lets kids be kids.

The children's line uses a wider range of color and is worn much looser than the adult styles. However, the luxury appeal is maintained through the use of fur trim, thick sweaters, and the velvety qualities of corduroy. In reading the ad in Figure 4.5, the viewer notes the celebration of diversity. It is clear that the company believes that children should be allowed to embrace their individuality. Most notably, not all boys should have short hair (*left*) and not all girls need to wear cute dresses (*center*). The children in this ad do not all have the same body type. They are *real children* who just happen to wear D&G Junior clothing. The ad represents D&G children's fashions as practical with an artistic flair.

The men's line is also advertised in typical Dolce & Gabbana style. The ad in Figure 4.6 shows some men who are professionally dressed and others who are more casual. The models are very sexy. In this ad, Dolce & Gabbana reinforces the notion that its male customer is not afraid to be his own man, wearing whatever emulates sex appeal. By placing a snake on a clearly objectified model in the center of the photo, Dolce & Gabbana suggests that its male customer could fall under the temptation of the right person or the "Eve to their Adam." Whether this Eve is female or male needs further discussion. In addition to the

FIGURE 4.5 The models in advertisements for the D&G children's line reflect nontraditional gender characteristics.

Adam and Eve reference, the snake can be deciphered to represent sneakiness, cruelty, or danger. Or, taking it further, the snake could represent the character of the reclining male bather, who could be the snake between the two on either side of him. However, the idea of a female Eve is reinforced by the female legs on the diving board. On the other hand, the male body in the foreground is holding a drink that may be meant for the reclining model, suggesting that the two are a couple. The woman, reclining male, and male standing with glass in hand seem to be engaged in a triangular discourse, unlike the rest of the figures in the photo, who are simply decoration.

Analyzing the Adam and Eve idea further, because Dolce & Gabbana are Italian, the biblical references in their ads come from the highly Catholic culture in which they were raised. The Catholicism of the designers is also illustrated in Figure 4.1, with the crucifix that Domenico Dolce wears around his neck. Also, the earlier quote about the company's female customer refers to the Communion rosary worn as a necklace, which leads this author to conclude that both men may be influenced by the Catholic religion.

The ad in Figure 4.6 also illustrates the diversity among male consumers, who are willing to take fashion risks. Unlike most menswear ads that show men in boring suits, this ad has each man wearing something different. Dolce & Gabbana truly believe that theirs should be the brand that men wear in every aspect of life.

FIGURE 4.6 What is the story behind this 2007 advertisement for Dolce & Gabbana menswear?

The Future of Sparkle and Shine

Dolce & Gabbana are leaders in luxury branding. With sales in the millions, these two men have created a global lifestyle brand. But how will they maintain the image of exclusivity? Was that ever their goal? Is Dolce & Gabbana an exclusive brand, or have people just assumed this because of the high price tag on their products?

By targeting consumer markets such as the gay and lesbian community as well as affluent sectors of society, and by dressing *real* women and featuring them in their ads, Dolce & Gabbana are making a statement. This design team focuses on building the brand-to-customer relationship with *all* people; being exclusive and restrictive is too conservative for them. The types of individuals featured in Dolce & Gabbana ads reflect this individualistic attitude. For example, Dolce & Gabbana may have chosen Brooke Shields in 1995 for an advertising campaign simply because she was the best celebrity endorser, or because she represents someone who has endured and maintained her personal integrity. Brooke Shields has challenged the norms of society as an actress and model. In 1978, at the age of thirteen, Shields played a child prostitute in the movie *Pretty Baby*. The backlash from this movie nearly destroyed her career. But in 1980, Calvin Klein used Shields in a jeans ad with the tagline, "You want to know what comes between me and my Calvins? Nothing." This ad also caused controversy, but Shields survived the onslaught and established herself as one of the most recognizable celebrities in the world.

By featuring a strong, extraordinary woman like this, Dolce & Gabbana challenged the social order that has traditionally applied to fashion. They stated that it is not just the "prim and proper" that deserve luxury fashion, but *all* consumers, regardless of their personal life, and that is really what their brand message is all about. Dolce & Gabbana have attained their current stature by dressing fashion's risqué misfits, featuring individuals who are unique, sexy, and unusual, as well as gays and lesbians, *real* woman, diverse children, and those not normally included in fashion advertising. Unlike Ralph Lauren, who dresses a more traditional, uptight, conservative, and restrictive customer, Dolce & Gabbana dress the ostentatious. Their customers genuinely admire what the brand stands for in the global fashion marketplace. These two men will continue to be fashion's fairy godmothers, dressing those that everyone else has ignored. With a wave of their wands, they will make us sparkle, shine, and appear *fantastically sexy!*

Discussion Questions

1. Currently, how many divisions do Dolce & Gabbana have in their company? Has it grown since this chapter was written? If so, how?
2. Do you think Dolce & Gabbana cater to the fashionistas that the rest of the design world has rejected? Why do you think they have dressed women like Isabella Rossellini, Madonna, Kylie Minogue, and Brooke Shields? Do you think these women are risqué? Why or why not?
3. Do you think gay and lesbian consumers purchase different fashion brands than heterosexuals? Do you think it was smart for Dolce & Gabbana to target this market? Why or why not?

Exercise

In this chapter you discovered that Dolce & Gabbana are known for their unique advertising campaigns. How well can you *read* (or analyze) one of their ads or any other fashion ad? Find a fashion ad and share with your colleagues all the innuendos you find hidden in the ad. How does this ad reflect culture or history? Does the ad say anything about the particular brand? What is subliminally suggested? Back up your thoughts with reasons from history, culture, or contemporary ideas.

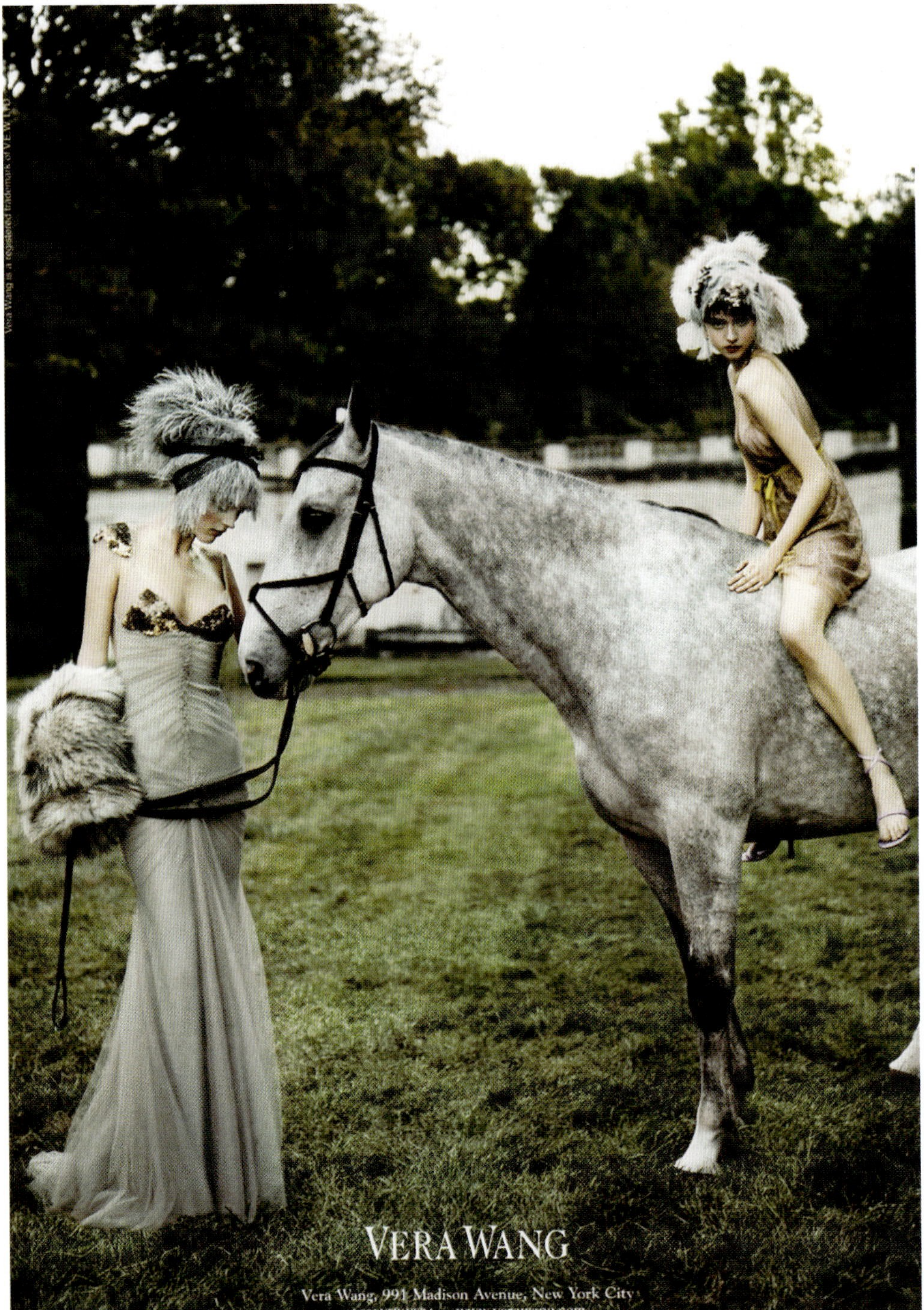
Vera Wang is a registered trademark of V.E.W. Ltd.
VERA WANG
Vera Wang, 991 Madison Avenue, New York City
1.800.VEW.VERA
www.verawang.com

CHAPTER FIVE

THE EMPRESS OF FASHION

VERA WANG

From Fifth Avenue to Simply Vera

In 1991 Vera Wang founded a design company that reflects her lifelong love of fashion and celebrates the romance, sensuality, and spirit of modern young women. She took the simple idea of designing her own wedding dress and, in fewer than 20 years, turned it into a multimillion-dollar company that now includes a deluge of products and home accessories that reflect an elaborate lifestyle brand. The wonderful success of Vera Wang comes from her talent for creating storybook weddings and her practical experiences as a former *Vogue* editor and Ralph Lauren merchandiser. The latter roles equipped her for creating a successful mass-marketed line of products for Kohl's department stores. Wang is an international design magnate whose products maintain a brand image of elegance, no matter where they are sold. Her career is a guide for all who study or want to work in fashion; the "road to success" has many twists and turns, but maintaining focus and integrity will surely lead to triumph.

Vera Wang: Wedding Expert and Role Model

Vera Wang started her business in 1991, when she was unable to find a dress for her own wedding ceremony. She designed one herself and since then has redefined the concept of wedding dresses and the entire ceremonial package. She designs and has licensing agreements for everything from couture wedding gowns to bridesmaid dresses, lingerie, china, stemware, flatware, barware, home décor, fine paper products, four different fragrances, and she has even written a book. Not only does Wang provide the perfect wedding dress with all the accoutrements, she can even supply a place for the wedding couple to sleep, through a licensing agreement with Serta mattresses. Apart from her wedding-related products, Wang has joined the ranks of fashion designers who have branched out to big-box retailing with a mass-marketed line of reasonably priced clothing, called Simply Vera.[1] Vera Wang's clear vision for her company continues to foster its growth.

Vera Wang is a role model for today's young fashionistas. Her career path reflects a woman who is educated, cultured, and able to transfer skills from one area of expertise to another. Retail consolidations, industry mergers, and changes in other fashion arenas have contributed to an environment in which it is quite possible that many who work in the fashion industry will have to move from job to job. Students of fashion, retailing, and merchandising sometimes expect to land their ultimate dream job as soon as they graduate from college. Although dreaming is wonderful and everyone needs goals, it should be kept in mind that it might take some time to attain them. Staying focused and pursuing your ultimate career is very important, but opportunities that may seem unrelated might come along and should not be ignored. You never know where the fashion path will lead you.

Vera Wang's career has evolved from the focused business strategy of creating *the best* wedding dress to licensing agreements and a mass-merchandised lifestyle line of fashion for woman throughout the United States. Vera Wang has created a fashion empire—from Fifth Avenue to Simply Vera.

Who Is Vera Wang?

The intensity of focus that has made Vera Wang a success in the fashion world also led her to prosper in other areas. She was born in New York City on June 27, 1949, to an affluent family. Her father, Cheng-Ching Wang, had found success in Asia by creating distribution routes for pharmaceutical companies after World War II. He wanted Vera to pursue a career in medicine or law; he never dreamed she would be a fashion designer. But Vera had a passion for the arts and design.[2]

Until the age of 19, Vera trained to be a figure skater. She competed in the 1968 U.S. Figure Skating Championships and was listed as a featured athlete in the January 8, 1968, issue of *Sports Illustrated*. Her love of fashion began with the designs for her skating costumes. She also visited high-end designer showrooms and runway shows with her mother, Florence Wang, and brother, Kenneth Wang. Vera's primary goal was to be an Olympic skater, but unfortunately she did not make the team.[3]

Vera Wang attended the Chapin School in Manhattan and then enrolled at Sarah Lawrence College. She spent some time at the Sorbonne in Paris, which is when she discovered her love of design. After her sophomore year at college, Vera gave up her figure-skating career and pursued a career in fashion and design.[4]

Eventually, Wang returned to the United States and interviewed for a position at *Vogue* magazine. To prepare herself for the position, she took typing lessons at The Betty Owen School in New York. At age 21, she was hired as a rover, or temporary assistant, for editor Polly Mellen. Wang did whatever they asked her to do, such as sweeping floors, providing yogurt for models, and getting coffee. She was a glorified gofer. But young Vera knew her enthusiasm and work ethic would pay off.

Wang was made the youngest editor that *Vogue* had ever employed at the age of 23. During her 16 years at *Vogue*, Wang attained the title of senior editor and design director for accessories.[5] She took a leave of absence from *Vogue* after interviewing for the position of editor-in-chief, the position that Anna Wintour currently holds. At age 34, Wang returned to Paris for two years and spent time decorating her apartment. When she returned from Paris, she resigned from her post at *Vogue*.

Wang transferred her experience as senior editor at the most popular women's magazine to begin her career in design. With her networking skills and contacts from *Vogue*, Wang was able to tackle the position of design director for Ralph Lauren accessories.[6] It was at Lauren that Wang discovered her interest in mass fashion design. She was able to transfer her research skills in the area of accessories to design. Ralph Lauren must have been honored to have Wang on staff, with her extensive knowledge of the women's accessories market, the current brands that were leaders at the time, and her expertise in fashion forecasting and merchandising.

Vera Wang's Branding Story

Vera Wang's branding story begins in 1989, when she and Arthur Becker planned their wedding. After all her years in top-level jobs in the fashion industry, it was through the search for the perfect wedding dress that Wang found her calling. She wanted a dress that was contemporary and reflective of current styles. She found the dresses in the target market were too dowdy, not in good taste, or just plain ordinary, which forced her to design her own dress.

The following year, she opened her own luxury salon in the Carlyle Hotel in New York, which featured a line of fashionable wedding dresses. The original boutique started a trend in modern wedding gown styles (Figure 5.1). Wang began to introduce gowns at various price points that represented a "good, better, and best" strategy. For example, a good Vera Wang dress can cost between $3,000 and $7,000, the Vera Wang Luxe Collection is priced from about $6,000 to $20,000, and a Vera Wang couture gown runs much more. For the couture customers, the bride usually consults with a chief designer and might even meet Vera Wang herself.

The Vera Wang style became the epitome of wedding fashion, worn by numerous celebrities. A very popular was the one designed for Jennifer Lopez when she married Marc Anthony in 2004. Other famous brides have included Jessica Simpson, Thalia, Avril Lavigne, Victoria Beckham, Jennifer Garner, Campbell Brown, Jeri Ryan, Uma Thurman, Mariah Carey, and Karenna Gore, just to name a few. And Vera Wang even designed a wedding dress for the most popular woman in popular culture—Barbie. Vera Wang was introduced to Hollywood through Sharon Stone when Stone wore a Vera Wang sarong on the red carpet. Holly Hunter wore a Vera Wang original when she won the Oscar for *The Piano*, Jane Fonda was outfitted and styled by Vera Wang when she reentered the scene after her divorce from

FIGURE 5.1 Vera Wang pictured with models wearing some of her wedding gown designs.

Ted Turner, and Charlize Theron made her first debut on the red carpet in a stunning Vera Wang halter gown. Theron was placed on the best-dressed lists that year.

Wang Builds Her Brand Name

In addition to the dresses, Wang's clients started to ask her to plan their weddings or to recommend certain types of accoutrements for the event. So she started designing hard lines (non-clothing items), among other things. These became licensed businesses for Vera Wang; her china and crystal are manufactured by Waterford Wedgwood, and her silver plates and glasses by Syratech. Her 2001 book titled *Vera Wang on Weddings* provides specifics for the ultimate wedding.

Wang also designed a line of fragrances as part of the Vera Wang branding image. They include Vera Wang, Sheer Veil, Princess, and Vera Wang for Men. All the fragrances are licensed through an exclusive deal with Coty. As with many high-end designers, mass-produced fragrances allow mass customers a chance to own a piece of Vera Wang's product line because many are priced at less than $100. These mass-produced international fragrances have sold in vast quantities. With an expanded business strategy and extra funds gained from fragrance sales, as well as licensing agreements with Waterford Wedgewood, Syratech, and Coty, Wang has been able to maintain the integrity of her wedding gowns while moving into other clothing lines.

Throughout her career Wang has maintained her passion for figure skating, designing costumes for figure skaters including Nancy Kerrigan and Michelle Kwan. It was Kerrigan who helped build Wang's brand by winning the 1994 Olympic Games while wearing a Vera Wang original. This white dress was modeled after the one Marilyn Monroe wore when she sang "Happy

Birthday" to President John F. Kennedy. The dress made Vera Wang a superstar in a whole new market.

In 2005, when the upscale department store Bergdorf Goodman installed a Vera Wang salon on the third floor of its flagship store on Fifth Avenue, Vera Wang had truly arrived in women's fashion. That same year the Council of Fashion Designers of America named Vera Wang the Womenswear Designer of the Year.

Wang then decided to design luxury products for mass public consumption. Through these new products Vera Wang's business would increase its sales from an annual sum of $15 million. In the fall of 2005 Vera Wang launched new lines of fine jewelry and luxe lingerie (Figure 5.2) that brought almost $300 million in retail store dollars. This success proved that the company had potential in the mass market and that consumers wanted more Vera Wang products. However, even these products were geared

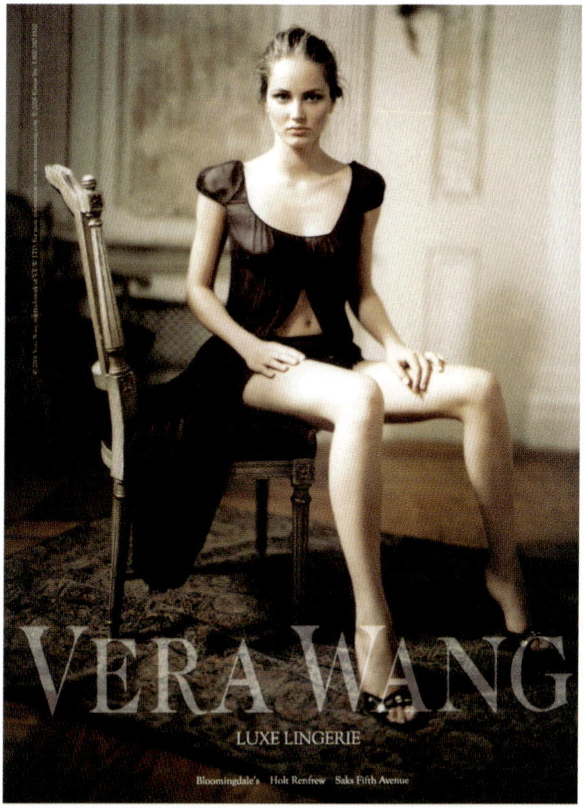

FIGURE 5.2 A 2006 advertisement for Vera Wang Luxe lingerie.

toward an upper-middle-class, affluent clientele. The company was not reaching larger audiences and gaining its dollar share of the mass market.

Wang began to think that her name needed to reach more than just the few high-end department store consumers who were buying her lines. In addition, she realized that the expensive goods she was designing would not allow everyone to have something that was Vera Wang. In her words, she realized "that few women really can afford a $2,000 dress, so I would love to design clothing that people can actually afford."[7]

Vera Wang Goes to Kohl's

On Sunday, September 9, 2007, Vera Wang launched her Simply Vera product line at Kohl's department stores nationwide at 749 locations. This collection, through a long-term licensing agreement with the Menomonee, Wisconsin retailer, featured sportswear, intimate apparel, handbags, leather accessories, jewelry, footwear, bed linens, and towels (Figure 5.3).[8]

The price points for the line reflect a very moderate range, with dresses ranging from $70 to $100 and other products at prices similar to those found at retailers such as Gap. The clothing is extremely well designed, and the fashionable style reflects the Vera Wang brand. She states it best:

> For me, Simply Vera, Vera Wang represents not just a fashion philosophy, but a vision about life and style. It's also a true expression of my own personal design vocabulary . . . the deliberate mixing and matching of different weights, colors, and textures . . . layering for charm, style, and comfort . . . relaxed shapes and silhouettes with subtle artistic flourishes. I also love an element of surprise here and there, a touch of the unexpected. Details on a dress can inspire bed linens, and jewelry or embellishments can adorn a bag

FIGURE 5.3 A Simply Vera ensemble. This reasonably priced line is available through Kohl's department stores.

or a shoe. This juxtaposition of ideas speaks to a modern sensibility that is fun, easy, and sophisticated.

Casual can be stylish, dressy can be casual. From the runway to the red carpet, the aisle to the home, my hope is that SimplyVera, Vera Wang gives women the confidence to express their own personal style.[9]

The Vera Wang company has many leading branding partners that ensure that the line maintains its integrity. This company is dedicated to designs that reflect the true Vera Wang style—sophistication, simplicity, and perfection. The company has over 200 employees who create the bridal gown collection in U.S. work rooms. The detailing required to make these gowns is labor intensive, but the company maintains a high level of production by hiring the best designers and seamstresses. As a student who worked for Vera Wang said, "Everyone is treated very well. Vera is great and she demonstrates hard work with humility. She is very professional and gives wonderful feedback. When you work for Vera Wang you know that you are respected for your talents and skills."[10]

INTERVIEW

Training Employees is Crucial! Talking with Michelle Bakar the Human Resources Operations Manager for the Coles Group/Wesfarmers in Australia.

Vera Wang did not create a multinational conglomerate by herself. She relies on her employees to understand her dreams and ideas for the brand and to aid her in maintaining her vision. Great companies have to train their employees on how to execute strategy. This is particularly important in the luxury market where the clients and the customers are usually more educated and a "tougher sell." Michelle Bakar, the Human Resources Operations Manager for the Coles Group/Wesfarmers, a mass grocery retailer in Australia, spoke with the author about the importance of effective training for retail organizations. Ms. Bakar has a Master of Science degree in marketing and doctorate in communications and branding. Her years of experience in marketing and retail led to her present position with Coles, where she focuses on talent development and cultural strategy. She has extensive knowledge in employee training and development for both the luxury and mass markets.

How important is it to properly train employees about the company brand?

If the employee does not epitomize and understand the values of the company, then the company should not expect its customers to understand its brand proposition and become passionate about the company's products. Training and sales go hand in hand, particularly in fashion, which is very much about the brand helping the customer rationalize needs and wants (identification), a brand personality can be the differential. "I NEED those Gucci shoes" as opposed to "I WANT those Gucci shoes!!" If an employee can effectively explain the personality and identity of a brand to a customer, then it's like introducing a potential lover or best friend. Employees need to be clear about the brand message, and be able to communicate those clearly to the customer. Training should be about heritage, the journey of the brand, the target market, and how the employee can target the customer to gain a sale. It can also be about helping the employees translate the message into feelings so that they pass this on to the customer. Selling techniques in the spirit of the company are absolutely essential to its reputation. The clothes are the product. Selling is the technique. The brand message is the feeling. Effective training in these areas will guarantee better customer service, customer and employee satisfaction, and of course, profit and business growth.

Do you think employees are an important link in the big picture of a fashion brand?
Great customer service is about helping a consumer understand how an item will enhance his or her lives. The employee needs to live and breathe the brand for that aspiration to pass on to the customer. I always asked my staff, "Would you wear this? Would your friends want to buy this?" If they are not passionate, they won't be right for the business. You can teach skill, but you can't teach passion; so start with someone who believes in the brand, then train him or her in the

brand's history and ensure he or she has the right tools to go and do a fantastic job. They must also feel like they represent the brand, so benefits and remuneration must also reflect the company vision as well as a top-class performance appraisal and feedback program. If your managers do not value their teams, then you can forget about the strategy being successful; if your managers are not excited about the employees' welfare within a company (which IS the company), then revenue will stagnate; a company is only as good as the people behind it and if your company is full of smart, savvy, passionate individuals who take pride in their roles and in their product, then the business will flourish.

Good strategies for happy employees include rewards and remuneration and processes, but also meaning and difference from an HR perspective. For example, when I worked for Ella Baché, a luxury cosmetic company, Chairman John Hallas directed all employees to take a paid day-off each month to work at a charity of their choice. Instead of losing productivity, which was a potential risk, it attracted a deluge of people wanting to work for the company. It could have been any company, not just a luxury brand. Get the employees involved and empowered, and they will take ownership and accountability.

Are the corporate employees or the in-store employees more important when it comes to communicating the brand to the customer?

The corporate employees are always there to support the in-store people, so both are linked. The marketing team creates the overall brand and product strategy as well as the local strategies to the end customer (product, price, place, promotion). The trainers educate about the product and techniques; the front-line staff runs with the promotional strategy and makes revenue. [Their] importance is equal, and the end customer must always receive a very consistent message from when they walk into a store to the smile on the sales assistant's face.

What do you think will be the future of fashion branding? Should universities be teaching students about fashion branding?
Fashion branding is important for future fashion designers and anyone who wants to work in fashion because it is the study of brand personality and all the components that go into the business creation of an image. The subject is intriguing and potent, and being able to look at it critically will help us understand and [get] leverage from the way society thinks, feels, and reacts. Universities that teach humanities should look at how dress and adornment affects culture. Business faculties can also look at the powerhouses of fashion labels and their persistent survival via leadership, marketing, and finance. Design faculties should add fashion branding to their practical components because young designers need to be informed and aware when they make design decisions on how to get their designs out to market in the way they intended. Students need to look at fashion critically. Branding studies are essential.

In your own words, what is fashion branding?
Fashion branding refers to the business and communications process behind the creation of a brand's personality. This includes trends, tactics, techniques, strategy, mission, and values. It is also very much about understanding cultural codes, appropriation, representations of the body, and ways of seeing fashion.

Do you have any advice for those who wish for a career like yours?
If you love style, if you love fabrics, design, and the way clothes are worn, or if you love high-end luxury fashion, then capitalize on it by creating a career for yourself. Understand what your skills are (and aren't) and write yourself a job description. Get educated so you have a unique point of difference. Then target the brands you love and network your way in. Fashion loves entrepreneurialism. Make yourself trendy! In this way, you'll be happy with your job in an industry that you will love for the rest of your life!

The Career Continues

Fashion is Vera Wang's passion. She has dedicated her life to becoming a leader in the industry and is an excellent role model for anyone who aspires to succeed in business. She has proven that you can pursue your dreams and reach your ultimate goal. Although many critics have stated that Wang had it easy because of her father's money, she would not have attained this level of success without passion, focus, and drive. Vera Wang works hard and is loyal to her brand.

The company continues to grow and may well be on the way to becoming a global brand. With products that range from couture fashions to bed linens, the future looks bright for Vera Wang's empire.

Discussion Questions

1. In what way is Vera Wang a great example of the ever-changing career path of an individual?
2. Go to www.verawang.com. What changes have occurred in the company since the writing of this chapter? Has the brand expanded into other products?
3. In your own words describe the Vera Wang brand. How does

this brand differ from others, such as Ralph Lauren or Dolce & Gabbana?

Exercise

It is time for some self-reflection by answering the following questions: What are your professional plans for the future? How do you intend to make those plans happen? What stumbling blocks do you think you will have to clear along the way? How long do you think it will take to reach your goals?

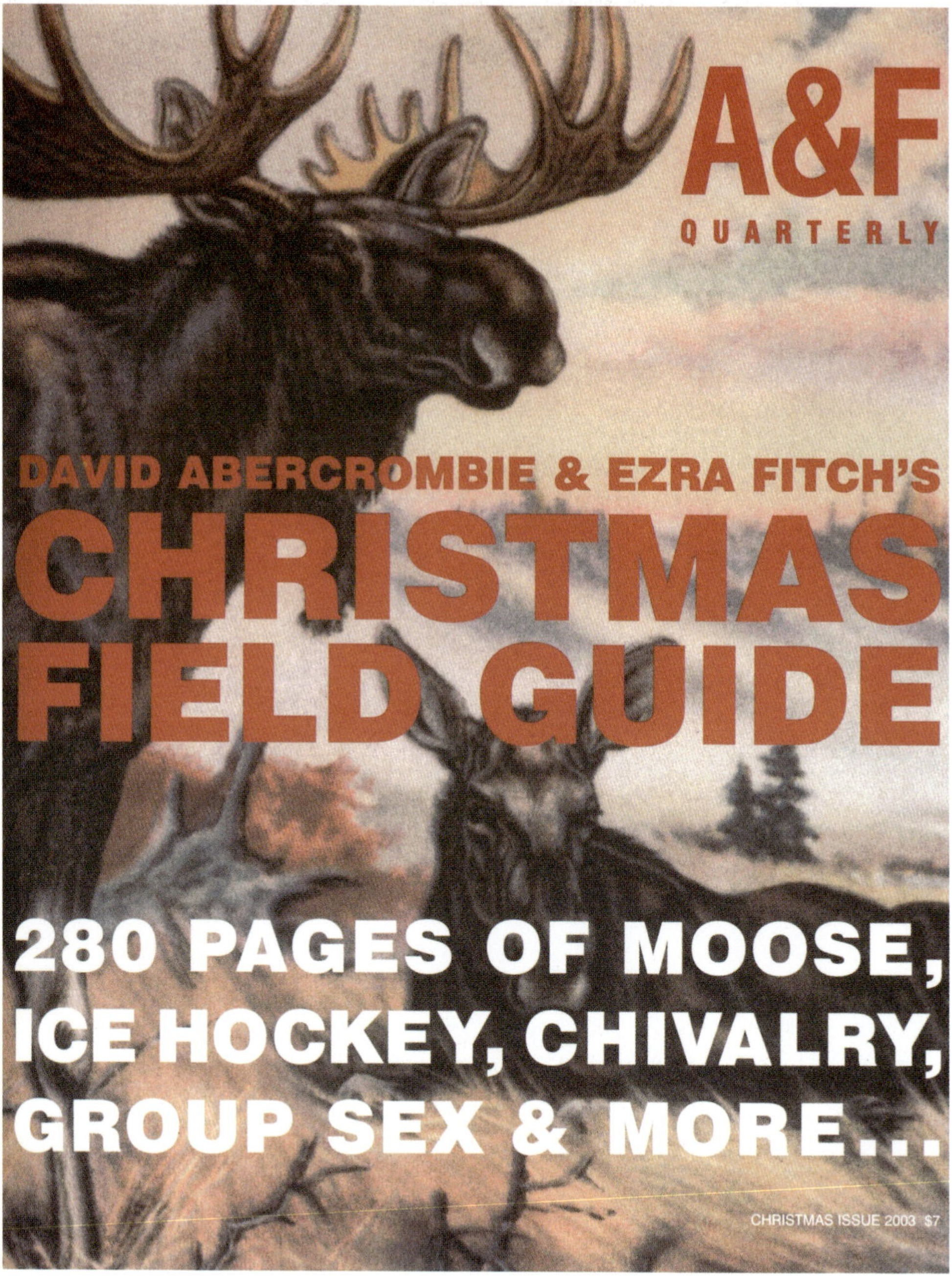
A&F
QUARTERLY
DAVID ABERCROMBIE & EZRA FITCH'S
CHRISTMAS
FIELD GUIDE
280 PAGES OF MOOSE,
ICE HOCKEY, CHIVALRY,
GROUP SEX & MORE...
CHRISTMAS ISSUE 2003 $7

CHAPTER SIX

IN-STORE BRANDING CONCEPTS

ABERCROMBIE & FITCH

From Safari Gear to Shirtless Hunks

Abercrombie & Fitch (A&F) is the ultimate example of branding as an experience; the brand permeates the stores. The dim lighting, smell of fragrance, and booming music exude youth. The image is casual luxury. This in-store branding concept has led to multimillion-dollar sales of T-shirts, denim jeans, and cargo shorts year after year; everyone from middle-school students to athletically fit adults loves the trim silhouettes. Some culturally diverse groups such as the gay and lesbian community admire A&F's store concept, whereas ethnic minorities have criticized its in-store marketing campaigns. The stores themselves seem exclusive. Entering an A&F store is a lot like walking into a nightclub that just happens to sell clothes. Newspaper reporters, academics, and parents have continually noted that the store is over the top; yet the company has had continued success. Chief Executive Officer Michael Jefferies was often noted in the *Daily News Record* as someone who truly knows fashion. The retailer has extended to the international market and plans continued growth through its various divisions.

This company has proven that if you sell a great product and create a great atmosphere, you can become a leader in fashion. A&F dictates its own casual luxury and style.

The A&F Lifestyle

The David T. Abercrombie Company was founded in 1892 as a retail outlet carrying high-quality camping, fishing, and hunting gear. The early clientele consisted of avid sportsmen, including a New York lawyer by the name of Ezra Fitch. Abercrombie and Fitch became partners in 1904. The two men had different ideas about the store's image, and Abercrombie left the company in 1907. In the 1920s, Ezra Fitch's 12-story Madison Avenue store served affluent outdoorsmen (and women), including Theodore Roosevelt and Amelia Earhart.

The company struggled for a number of years and was eventually bought by the Limited Corporation in 1988, who reinvented A&F to reflect a new contemporary image (Figure 6.1). In 1998, A&F separated from The Limited to become an independent retailer. By the first quarter of 2007, the company encompassed 4 divisions and 947 stores: A&F stores targeted 18- to 22-year-olds in 355 locations; 180 A&F stores focused on the children's market (7- to 14-year-olds); Hollister Co. for teenagers aged 14 to 18 years operated 396 stores; and Rheul No. 925 had 16 stores targeting adults aged 23 to 35 years. A&F envisions itself as the "Creator and Operator of Aspirational Lifestyle Brands."[1] The company plans to continue its growth into Canada, Europe, and Japan.

The corporate officers of the company pride themselves on having total control over stores, fashion design, sourcing, pricing, and marketing. A&F believes it offers the consumer excellent quality and key trends, and prides itself on the capability to sell products at full retail price. The company continues to focus

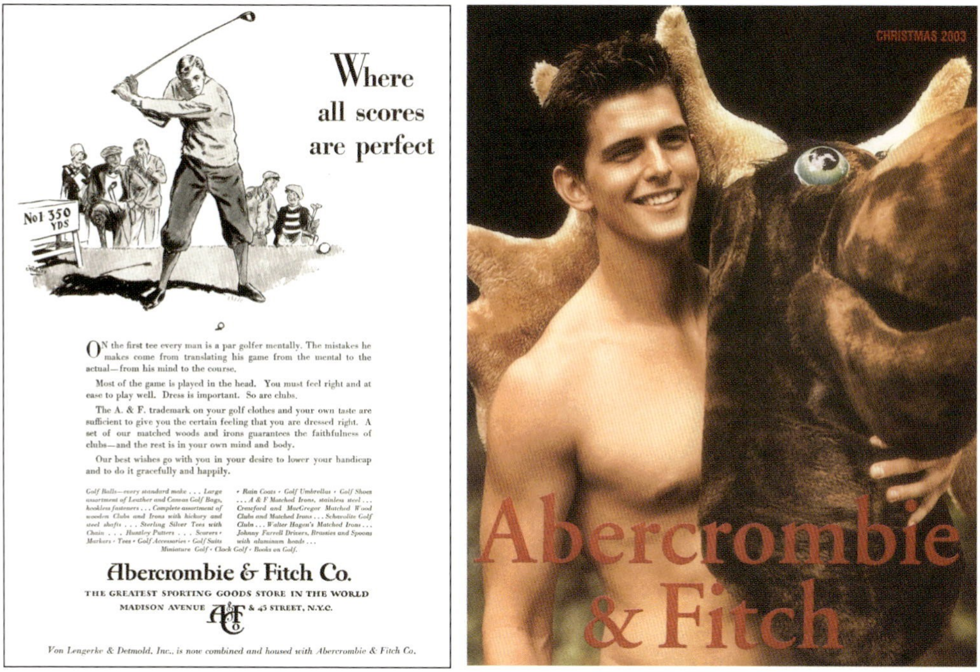

FIGURE 6.1 The historical Abercrombie & Fitch was geared toward traditional sporting goods (*left*), but after the Limited purchased the company it began to focus more on youth culture and mass fashion (*right*).

on first-rate price levels with higher priced and better quality products reflecting A&F's *casual luxury* theme.

The company's fashion assortment consists of basic items such as cargo shorts and pants, T-shirts (logo, humor Ts, and crewnecks), polo shirts, woven shirts, sweaters, denim jackets, jeans, sweatshirts, zip fleece tops, leather belts, flip-flops, underwear, cologne, baseball caps, men's and women's bracelets and jewelry, bags, and various other types of activewear. A&F took basic garments and made them its own. Almost every item at A&F is made to look worn and washed out. Also, the retailer has refitted items such as oxford shirts, T-shirts, and polo shirts with more body-conscious fashion silhouettes; for example, a T-shirt has become a muscle-T, whereas traditional garments such as oxford and polo shirts have the word *muscle* sewn into the label of the garment.

Controversial Branding Strategies

A&F attaches traditional outdoor and rugged iconic patches on sweaters, pants, and denim garments, which have allowed the retailer to gain strong brand recognition. Symbols such as collegiate flags, sports mascots, and the letters A&F appear on almost all products. The company has even adopted the logo of a moose that it embroiders on all its polo shirts and oxfords. Almost every garment at A&F is imbued with washing, styling, and distressing that distinguishes it as authentic A&F. The company brands each garment through this finishing process.

A&F has created a merchandising concept for its stores that is unique and easily distinguishable from its competition. It maintains constant market share through product positioning, merchandise categories, and continued growth in other markets. Since the mid-1990s, A&F's 61-year-old CEO Michael Jeffries has contributed to all of the company's marketing endeavors.

The company has been surrounded by controversy over its homoerotic and naked coed marketing; however, retail sales indicate that consumers continue to shop A&F stores in spite of the criticism. The company promotes its sex-driven image and continues to perpetuate erotic play with every new advertising campaign. In his book *The Erotic History of Advertising* Tom Reichart states, "Abercrombie is to fashion what *Maxim* is to magazines . . . both are extremely profitable, enjoying exponential sales increases, and both use skin to appeal to teens and young adults."[2]

To say that A&F has caught the attention of the press would be an understatement. A&F ads are created by the well-known gay fashion photographer Bruce Weber. The marketing campaigns are infused with male homoeroticism, which reflects the sexual orientation of Weber and CEO Jeffries. In addition, ads glorifying young semi-nude bodies of both sexes dominate the promotional images of almost every season. Whereas the press as well as academics have criticized these images of the nude body (among other issues), the homosexual community has embraced the sexual freedom of the company's advertising strategy.

Even today, this youth-obsessed marketing, which features predominantly masculine themes, has been a key to A&F's success in the retail market. It was during the late 1990s that A&F's marketing strategy gained momentum with promotions geared toward college coeds, the gay community, and other A&F enthusiasts. The Abercrombie *magalogue*, as it was referred to in the *The Wall Street Journal* on July 29, 1997, was popular and became more than a mail-order catalogue; it was a lifestyle guide for thousands of consumers.[3] These photographic magalogues have become collector's items and are sold on the eBay website for more than $100 each. Even today, some collectors continue to feature these marketing magalogues among their traditional art books, which indicates that A&F's magalogues are also viewed as works of art and popular culture artifacts. Although the publication was effective as a promotional device, many conservative activist groups protested the magalogue's use of blatant group sex scenes and homoerotic themes in order to sell items such as cargo pants and muscle-Ts. An article by David Reines titled "All the Nudes That's Fit to Print" cites A&F's magalogue as sexually charged and reveals how the American Decency Association and other groups called for a national boycott of the retailer.[4]

As Greg Lindsay states, "The Quarterly made Abercrombie's name synonymous with a neo-preppy look found in its clothes and the all-American perfection of its models, but its edgy tone and imagery drove critics (and there were many) over the edge."[5] This suggests that it definitely was not the clothing that made A&F unique, but the branding. Even the Slovenian philosopher Slavoj Zizek has graced A&F's magalogues with his philosophical advice. In the 2003 back-to-school edition, Zisek wrote the copy for the summer edition of Abercrombie's marketing campaign. Another prominent academic, Dwight McBride, the chairman of the African American studies department at Northwestern University, has been so outraged by A&F's image of "whiteness" and lack of blacks in its ads and stores that he titled one of his books *Why I Hate Abercrombie & Fitch.*[6] Since the book's publication in 2005, Abercrombie has readjusted its workforce and advertising campaigns to address ethnic diversity; however, most of the in-store marketing still features white collegiate men.

The Retail Store as Brand

In their book *Experiential Retailing: Concepts and Strategies That Sell*, Youn-Kyung Kim, Pauline Sullivan, and Judith Cardona Forney propose that it is the shopping experience that keeps customers interested in retailers. Although the products are important, what people really desire is to be entertained when they are buying their khaki pants and T-shirts.[7] In his book *Branding a Store*, Ko Floor reveals that the retail store setting is where items are contextualized and given product identity. According to Floor, the store design is a communication tool for the shopper, and it is within this space that values of the brand are created, adding contextual ideology to the product assortment and creating a perceived lifestyle.[8]

One objective of most retailers is to create stories, narratives, or myths that are reflective of popular culture, to entice consumers to purchase their products.[9] Often, merchandise collections are given theme or story names that reflect the seasons or lifestyle events, such as *nautical, country, back-to-school, holiday,* or *spring break.* Through narration and contextualization of these products, possible connections to historical, contemporary, cultural, or personal events could be triggered in the mind of the consumer.[10] A retailer needs to relate to the consumer in a method that is clear and understandable. By combining the product in the context of the retail store, the theme or storyline is easily understood.

INTERVIEW

The "Total" Store Image Fosters a Fashion Brand's Success: Talking with Lynn McGrane

Even with the Internet, brick-and-mortar stores are still an important component for most fashion brands. Whether it is a specialty retailer like A&F or a department store like Bloomingdale's, there is pressure on store managers to maintain a "brand-right" image for the customers. Retailing is not a job; it is a career, and only the most talented make it into top management positions. Lynn McGrane is Vice President and General Manager for Bloomingdale's in King of Prussia, Pennsylvania. Over the course of a more than 35 years she has observed and engaged in every aspect of luxury retailing.

How important is fashion branding to a luxury retailer like Bloomingdale's?

By definition, fashion branding is especially important in luxury retail. The consumer looks for characteristic consistency of product, which includes quality, image, and what the brand stands for and represents. Luxury brands rely on branding to support price and reputation. At times, when the customer is more aware of purchasing, especially in luxury goods, the brands that have been purchased with satisfaction, or that have a solid reputation, will survive and thrive.

As time goes by, do you see fashion branding becoming more or less significant?
I believe fashion branding will be more important. As the choices for consumers continue to grow, that status of owning trending brands will also continue. The brand may initiate the trend by creating a supply and demand issue, or may drive exclusivity by limiting the number of stores where it may be sold. This creates the beginning of the important relationship between a retail store and the fashion brand. Fashion branding is here to stay. One purpose of branding is to develop loyalty from the consumer. In our culture, time is a precious commodity. Stores focus on time efficiency by expedient service . . . carrying successful brands that marry to the store's brand is crucial. And the consumer, who knows that particular fashion brand, has confidence in that purchase. For the retailer, it secures sales.

Is it difficult for a luxury retail store like Bloomingdale's to convey the right image to the consumer?
When a store partners with the fashion brand, negotiations must include understanding the needs of that brand, visuals, presentation, product knowledge, and marketing. Because most fashion brands have clearly established their own vision, it becomes a matter of agreement. Some stores are unwilling to alter the architecture or signage, some fashion brands will not compromise their vision of presentation, including fixtures, wall color, or signage. So the amount of time varies based on these points, but when both brands involved work in earnest, it generally works.

How important are sales associates and store managers in the role of fashion branding?
The selling professionals are *vitally* important because they represent the store brand. And when they also represent a specific vendor or fashion brand, they must be educated and

passionate about that brand as well. Product knowledge is extremely important. A level of service commensurate with the brand is equally important. All of this reinforces both brands, which builds consumer loyalty. The general manager's role is to also understand the relationship between the fashion brand and the store's brand. They must communicate regularly the changes in fashion trends and ensure the importance and understanding of each vendor, especially in luxury brands.

Is the store's atmosphere important to the right brand image?
The store's atmosphere is critical to successful selling of fashion brands. Especially with luxury brands, the consumer has an expectation for an environment that supports this upscale merchandise. Lighting, cleanliness, fitting rooms, as well as presentation, signage, and visuals are considered. The entire store must reflect this level of merchandise to successfully build a rapport with the consumer who shops luxury brands. And again, the level of service, coupled with selling professionals who reflect this brand in their own appearance, is essential.

Do you have any advice for people who want to work in the world of luxury fashion brands?
Retailing is a business of passionate people. It offers many career options, but is always about people. My advice to anyone is to definitely consider a career in retailing. It is fast paced and exciting. The world of luxury retailing is one of partnerships and negotiation with constant change. There is much opportunity for job satisfaction.

A Trip to Abercrombie & Fitch

Examining the brand associates, the store design, in-store marketing, and atmospherics can help us to better understand how a company like A&F translates its visual brand advertising messages into a multisensory store experience that contextualizes its fashion-branded products. It is also important to be aware of how a mass retailer borrows from *narrative* and *cultural elements* that are reflective of popular culture to generate ideas and possibly gain sales.

Currently, all of A&F's stores are covered with wooden shutters (Figures 6.2 and 6.3). The four-story Fifth Avenue store in Manhattan is completely covered with the same shutters on each of its four floors. A customer only has to listen for techno dance music or catch a whiff of Fierce cologne (the company's signature scent) to find the A&F store in the mall.

What also draws the customer to the store are in-store marketing posters. At A&F, these are usually photos of attractive young men that get shoppers' attention. The darkened backdrop of the store (see Figures 6.2 and 6.3) enhances the in-store marketing and the ideology that this space might be exclusive or private. The combination of the shuttered façade, loud music, smell of cologne, and the visual of the poster give the customers a feeling that they are entering a distinctly stylish, exclusive, and perhaps a private space.

For the flagship store on Fifth Avenue, A&F has created a spectacle; two young male greeters on each side of the entrance welcome the customer. Currently, the company is using a multiethnic approach for gaining a wider target market and to reflect

FIGURE 6.2 Abercrombie & Fitch store in King of Prussia, Pennsylvania.

FIGURE 6.3 Abercrombie & Fitch store, Fifth Avenue, New York City.

that it is a diverse workplace. The A&F sales associates are stylized to look almost like twins. They speak to each other and sometimes greet customers. In Figure 6.4, the two greeters stand in front of A&F's Fall 2007 international in-store marketing poster of an exposed male pectoral draped by a flannel shirt. Contextualizing these brand associates in what appears to be a dark private space with loud music playing might suggest that these two men are bouncers in front of an exclusive nightclub or space.

The Shirtless Greeter

After you pass through the front doors at A&F you may see a shirtless "hunk" with a "hot" young female chaperone (Figure 6.5). In most high-volume and flagship stores (and every store during the peak seasons such as back-to-school and holidays), this young man greets you wearing only denim jeans and flip-flops (Figure 6.6). The shirtless A&F greeter models are accompanied by fully clothed female chaperones, who take photographs of the greeter with various patrons of the store.

In a role reversal of sorts, this clothed female greeter is not for sexual objectification, her male counterpart is clearly the target for that; rather, her purpose is to resolve levels of discomfort for various customers who may visit the A&F store. One of the most fragile categories is, perhaps, straight men. By allowing straight men to see that there is a beautiful female present, fear of homoeroticism is dissipated. Her presence also suggests that the shirtless model is straight and that she is *with him*, therefore, telling gay men "hands off." At the same time, she signals to straight men that by wearing A&F, you too might be accompanied by a "babe." Ironically, the muscled male greeter signifies to both men and women that this store *is* male space, thereby attracting men that might be intimidated by female space (think of your father entering Victoria's Secret) and elevating the status of A&F in the eyes of both sexes in our still very gender-conscious world. Certainly, the chaperone is there to make female customers feel comfortable. She allows women to see that the male model is there for *their* gaze, that A&F's women's assortment is great (by the way she is outfitted), and that this "stud" is friendly rather than predatory. She assures women that it is okay to visit A&F.

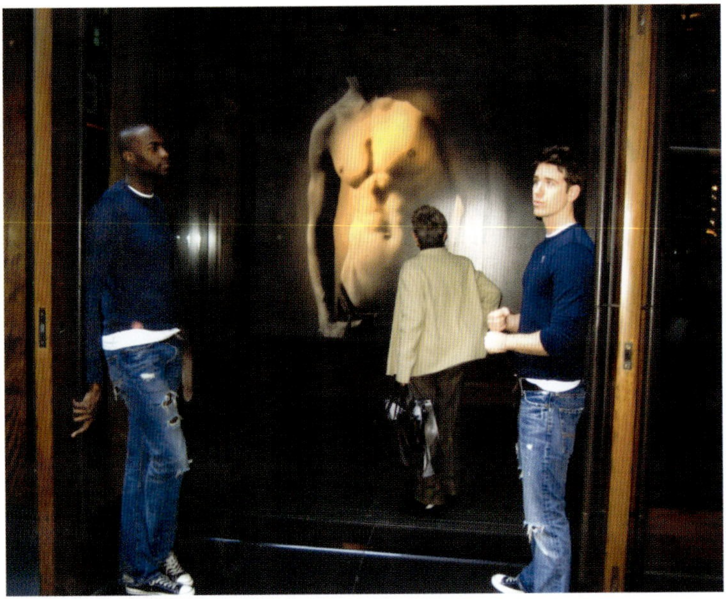

FIGURE 6.4 Abercrombie & Fitch Fifth Avenue store entrance. Note the greeters at either side of the main entrance.

FIGURE 6.5 A shirtless greeter and his female "chaperone."

The presence of shirtless greeters at A&F stores has generated a market niche for this company and reconnects them to the sexual innuendo that was present in the magalogues.

The Brand Associates

The Abercrombie brand associates, as the retailer refers to its salespeople, add to the stores' aura of exclusivity. Whether standing alone or "looking cool" by standing and modeling with one another, each associate is seen as mysterious; one of the secrets of the A&F brand. Servicing the customers in this space is not the priority. One look at the employees tells the customer that being fit and attractive is a prerequisite for working at A&F. Although women do work in the store, most of the brand associates are men, which suggests that the focus of the store is on the *maleness* of the retail brand.

These beautiful brand associates parody posing and dissin' in a hot nightclub. Many times these associates are standing and talking to each other; but customers cannot hear them because of the blaring house music. With the music, darkness of the store, the perfectly clothed muscle boys, and thin girls in tight Ts, denim, flip-flops, and large leather belts, a customer may be enticed to purchase A&F apparel just to be a part of this hotspot.

Branding Atmospherics

The mood for dancing is created with the store's blaring techno-house dance music. The company felt a loud sound was so crucial to its stores that it hired Meyer Sound, a professional sound company that was traditionally known for its work at popular dance clubs, to create the speakers.[11] The genre of music blasted in A&F reinforces the club atmosphere of the store. Its music mix mimics a list of songs that are played at the hippest clubs. This list includes songs from artists such as Erasure and Lucas Prata to the remixes of 1980s hits such as *The Glamorous Life* by Sheila E, *Rush Hour* by Jane Weidlin, or Belinda Carlisle's *Summer Rain*.

FIGURE 6.6 A shirtless greeter poses in front of a promotional poster.

The smell of A&F's signature fragrance, Fierce, fills the air. It, too, signifies the brand lifestyle and creates ties to the company's garments. Associates are told to spray the entire sales floor, including the clothing, with the fragrance. The smell creates a subliminal mindset for a consumer, a type of commercial aromatherapy designed to whet the appetite to buy cologne. The scent also creates a bond between the consumer and the image of A&F; those who want to accessorize to the minutest detail can purchase the cologne to make the A&F fantasy complete.

A&F also spreads its brand message by using consumers as *carriers;* the shopping bags and boxes feature shirtless men (and sometimes A&F-clad women). Consumers advertise the A&F brand to other shoppers by carrying the bags, which might entice others to visit the local A&F store.

The Masculinization of the Flagship Store

A flagship store is a premier location for a retailer. It represents the retail brand at the highest level of the branding strategy. More importantly, a flagship store is normally located in a city where many tourists may be exposed to a brand for the first time. Or they become more familiar with the brand because of the unique store location and design.

The A&F flagship store that opened in November 2005 on Fifth Avenue is a work of art (see Figure 6.3). A customer approaching this store knows he or she is in for a true shopping *experience*. The Fifth Avenue store (and two others in Grove City, California and London) is the ultimate salute to the A&F brand lifestyle.

From the sidewalk, customers are unable to see anything inside the store. On approaching the store, two men flanking the entrance greet the customer. When inside, the A&F shirtless model and his "chaperone" welcome the customer in front of the huge marketing poster. By this time the smell of Fierce cologne and the loud club music have been sensed. The first area a shopper views is the denim area of the store. A&F refers to this as the denim bar. On the women's side are female *denimtenders* and on the men's side are male denimtenders who are anxious to assist in finding the perfect pair of jeans.

After viewing the denim bar, the eyes of the customer are drawn to the crown molding, which features a scene of men and women that is reminiscent of the 1930s and 1940s (Figures 6.7 and 6.8). The mural is the work of artist Mark Beard and reflects his vision of the Ivy League lifestyle. As in most of A&F's marketing, there are very few women in the mural.

Beard was born in 1956 in Salt Lake City, Utah. Most of his work calls to mind a modern Michelangelo; he has been called a postmodern classical Greek artist. Like the Greeks, Beard focuses on the male form. A&F spared no expense when it hired the artist to create murals for its three flagship stores. The men's bodies in Beard's work are perfectly chiseled. Beard's other works, which include oil paintings, life drawings, ceramics, architectural elements, and bronze statues are shown at such venues as the Museum of Fine Arts in Boston and at Princeton, Harvard, and Yale Universities; more than a hundred private collectors own works by Beard.[12]

The main floor of the flagship store in New York resembles that of a traditional sporting goods store with a nightclub twist.

FIGURE 6.7 Interior of the Abercrombie & Fitch store on Fifth Avenue.

FIGURE 6.8 The Mark Beard mural in the Fifth Avenue Abercrombie & Fitch store.

A large fake moose head gives the perception that it was killed, stuffed, and mounted on the wall. Along the walls are old kayaks and boating oars. At the center of the main floor is a lit staircase. It is framed in steel and gives the aura of a work of industrial art and design. Along the walls of the staircase, from basement to ceiling, stretches the Mark Beard mural. The fitting rooms are darkened stalls very similar to those found at other A&F stores. It is very hard to see products in the fitting rooms, which forces customers to come out to see themselves.

Effective In-Store Branding

After viewing this flagship masterpiece, it is beyond a doubt that A&F has successfully tied its product to the store in its branding message. Its product line is similar to most lines by other mass merchants, such as Polo, J.Crew, or even Old Navy, but the store's context generates excitement about the product line. Although the company has created great controversy over its branding strategies, both in store and through advertising, it is clear that its processes work.

A&F has created a cultural brand through advertising narratives that generate feelings and emotions among consumers who view the ads and visit the stores. Whether these feelings are good or not does not matter, the company's branding and store design creates emotional responses in the consumer. Through the use of nude photography, shirtless male greeters, Fierce cologne, club mix house music, and the product, this brand is building future clients and dedicated followers. Its in-store strategy is simply ingenious.

By associating its brand to themes of masculinity, the company creates a triple threat to its competition: it draws the male customers who want to look like an A&F man, the woman who wants to resemble an A&F woman or who wants her boyfriend to look like an A&F man, and the overmasculinized look of the store and shirtless greeters gets the attention of gay men who feel the company is sympathetic to their lifestyle.

Whatever narrative a consumer receives when he or she walks into an A&F store, it is clear that this retailer is challenging notions of in-store branding. The company has pushed the buttons of some parents and others who may find its strategy offensive; however, this innovative company has built a reputation that is noted around the world.

Discussion Questions

1. Does A&F reinvent its brand strategy every year through its product assortment? Is it successful? Why or why not?
2. How does A&F brand its products? Do you think its brand practices are successful?
3. How do retail store atmospherics such as music, fragrance, lighting, store props, and retail brand associates strengthen a brand message? How do they weaken it?
4. What feelings or emotions do you experience when you enter an A&F store? Do you think A&F tries to intimidate its customer by using extremely attractive models?

Exercise

How do retailers convey their brand image through their retail stores? Visit a retail store and observe its atmospherics, store marketing, fixtures, customer service, and sales associates. Does the retailer convey a specific brand image to the customer? What is it? Is a story being told? How does the store space influence your opinions about the products being sold?

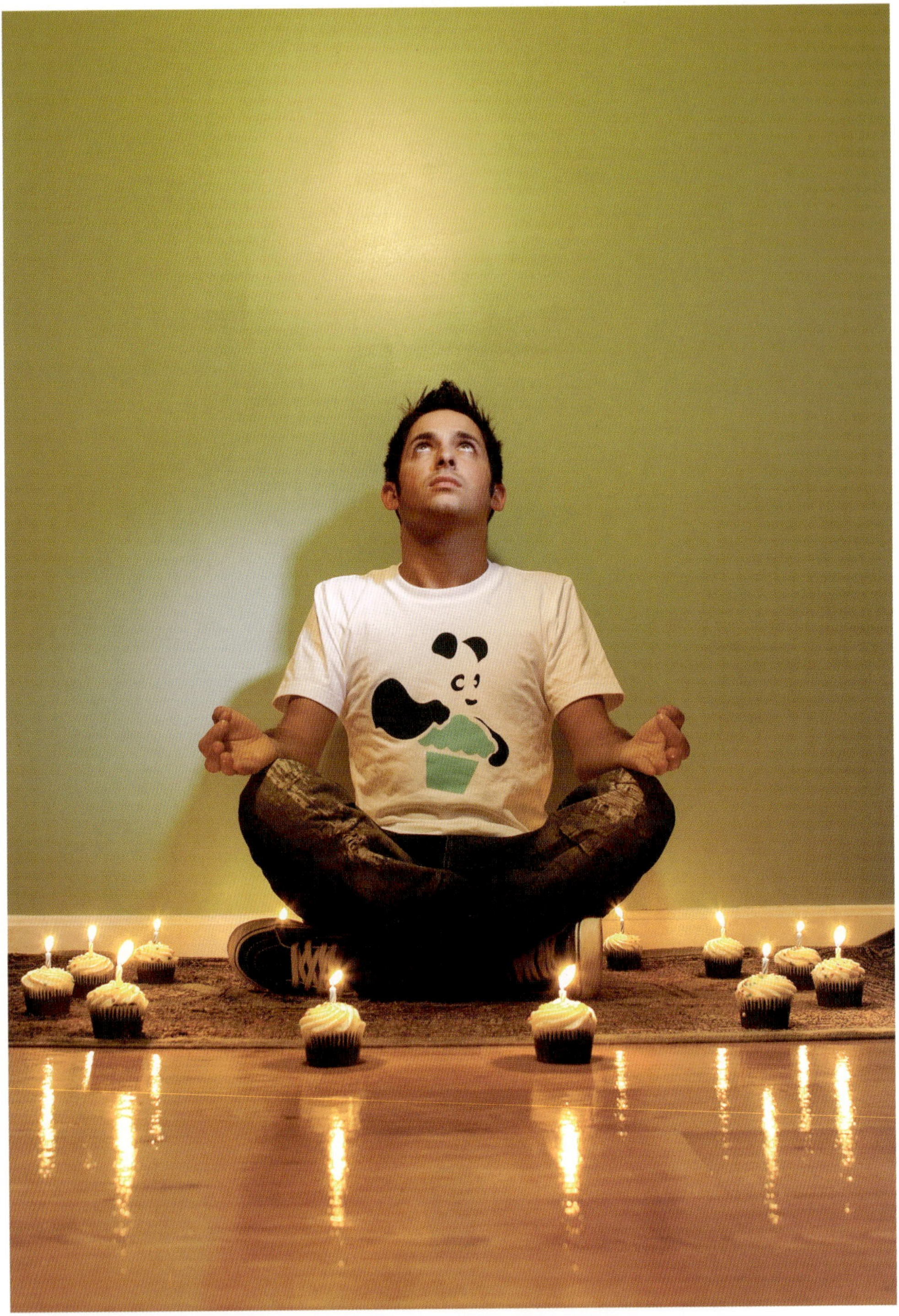

CHAPTER SEVEN

VIRAL FASHION BRANDING

JOHNNY CUPCAKES

Chasing Your Dreams!

The Johnny Cupcakes success story is extraordinary. By the ripe old age of 26, Johnny Cupcakes founder John Earle (who prefers to just be addressed as Johnny) had launched a multimillion-dollar company that continues to grow through a type of branding referred to as *viral fashion branding.* All of Johnny's fashion branding has been implemented through self-promotion, word of mouth, or by using electronic methods such as e-mail and the Internet. No pricey marketing firm has helped this young entrepreneur. Johnny Cupcakes has created a loyal customer base on his own terms.

Johnny's branding strategies have included the use of a blog (www.johnnycupcakes.com/blog/) where he shares his personal experiences and relates them to his brand. Bloggers can see his daily routine, his friends, his family, his personal associations with specific customers, and his own convictions concerning culture and society. This allows each person who visits the site to feel as if he or she is a part of his success. He knows exactly what he is doing and he is having fun doing it!

How Johnny Cupcakes Came to Be

While attending college to study music, Johnny (Figure 7.1) was distracted by the dream of owning his own business. He decided to leave school and focus on making his dream come true. So he went to work and eventually started a T-shirt business that skyrocketed him to success. His secret? Stay focused.

Johnny started his sales career in junior high school, selling what he called prank packs, which included items such as whoopee cushions, itching powder, and trick candy.[1] The T-shirt business started out as a joke while he was working at a comic shop (Newbury Comics) in Boston. A coworker of Johnny's gave him the nickname Johnny Cupcakes. The nickname stuck, inspiring Johnny to make a T-shirt with the nickname printed on the front. The T-shirt became a commodity coveted by friends, Newbury Comics customers, and strangers

FIGURE 7.1 Johnny Cupcakes wearing one of his hooded sweatshirts with the cupcake and crossbones logo.

on the street who wanted to know where he had purchased the T-shirt. Sometimes individuals came into Newbury Comics looking for the T-shirts. Johnny then began screen-printing copies of the shirt to sell out of the trunk of his car.[2]

Baking the Perfect Cupcake Tee

Johnny is an avid fan of popular culture and is influenced by symbols that influence youth and signify Americana. By using iconic figures on his first line of Johnny Cupcakes T-shirts, he was able to create stories associated with his new brand. For example, one of his shirts featured the Statue of Liberty holding a cupcake instead of a torch (Figure 7.2). Another T-shirt featured a jet plane, but instead of dropping parachutes it dropped cupcakes. Because the skull and crossbones symbol was popular when Johnny began designing, he decided to adopt a cupcake and crossbones as the company logo (see Figure 7.1).

In addition to being a salesman, Johnny was also a musician. He increased his target market when his band was on tour by having band members wear his T-shirts. He even took his

FIGURE 7.2 The suitcase that Johnny used to carry his wares when traveling from city to city. The assortment of T-shirts shown represents his early design concepts.

T-shirts with him on the road in an old beat-up suitcase (see Figure 7.2), and sold them to individuals and small boutiques.

In 2001, his band, On Broken Wings, signed a contract with a record label. This contract enabled Johnny to receive national exposure for his Johnny Cupcakes T-shirts. In his free time during concert tours, Johnny would take his suitcase of product to retail vendors and into shopping areas where he would sell them to anyone who showed an interest. Back home, Johnny's mom and younger sister would fill the orders. The entire family became part of the Johnny Cupcakes business.

When he returned home from each of his concert tours, Johnny would take what he had earned from T-shirt sales while on the road and reinvest it in the company. Each time, he would upgrade the quality of the fabric, trims, and screen-printing techniques. This pushed his T-shirts into a higher-quality market, giving them a better perceived value. This commitment to quality led to the current reputation of Johnny Cupcakes T-shirts as high-end products.

The demand for his products from fans of the band indicated to Johnny that the company was becoming successful.

> Some shows I'd sell more Johnny Cupcakes T-shirts than the band did with their merchandise. Not advertising or anything, these kids knew who I was and what I did. They'd search for me at every show. A strong Johnny Cupcakes following developed in just about every state. . . . I'd call it a cupcake-cult following. Kids that would collect every shirt, every colorway, et cetera. . . .[3]

But success can take a toll on family and personal life. The Johnny Cupcakes business started to monopolize Johnny's time. It was a strain to honor his obligation to the band while running the business, so Johnny decided to dedicate all of his time to the business and left the band.[4]

Cupcakes on the Internet

The Johnny Cupcakes Internet store was launched in 2002. The subsequent demand for T-shirts overwhelmed the family. His house became a warehouse for Johnny Cupcakes merchandise. Johnny states, "My parents had to literally move boxes in order to open the refrigerator, various closets, or to get to the bathroom."[5] With each new shipment, Johnny Cupcakes continued updating T-shirt styles and quality. Then the company took the next step to becoming a fashion-branded private label by sewing polyester satin tags into all the garments.

The company added surprises to the boxes when filling Internet orders.[6] Customers would find items such as trading cards that were popular in the 1980s and 1990s featuring Ninja Turtles, Ghostbusters, and Garbage Pail Kids, packed with their orders. These free trinkets were intended to make customers feel special and to help them remember the Johnny Cupcakes brand. As Johnny said, "It makes us stand out as a company and lets our customer know that we take the extra step to let them know we care."[7] Sometimes a vanilla scent is added to simulate the smell of baked goods. (The scent is also used in the Johnny Cupcakes stores.)

The unique screen prints that Johnny Cupcakes offers to customers have been noticed by the competition. Companies such as Urban Outfitters and Billabong have directly copied Cupcakes designs, forcing Johnny to take legal action. Although he is flattered by the copies, Johnny also believes that all companies should behave ethically.

In 2003, Johnny Cupcakes began to sell its products at men's fashion trade shows, such as the Men's Apparel Guild in California (MAGIC). Johnny Cupcakes T-shirts were first shown at the MAGIC menswear show in Las Vegas. A special catalogue was created for the show and the company representatives who attended wore chef's uniforms. The show was a success for Johnny Cupcakes; it secured orders for Japan, Italy, London,

Canada, and throughout the United States. Johnny Cupcakes was global!

While at the MAGIC tradeshow, another wonderful idea occurred to Johnny. He observed that many of the kids at the show wore the same cross-trainers. Johnny was stricken by the lack of exclusivity and uniqueness, and it was then and there that Johnny made the decision to create his shirts with limited supply runs. This means that only a certain quantity of each style is manufactured. Johnny also realized that he needed to be more exclusive in his distribution to retail outlets. So a limited group of retailers carries his product.

The company continued to grow through various marketing techniques. In 2004 it gave the first Cupperwear party at which Johnny lectured on how his business got started and the influences that inspire his T-shirt designs. After the talks, Johnny Cupcakes T-shirts are available for purchase by the audience.

The Oven Doors Open on Newbury Street

Because the viral fashion-branding techniques—concerts, word-of-mouth, the Internet, e-mails, tradeshow attendance, and Cupperware parties—had been successful for Johnny Cupcakes, the next logical step was a brick-and-mortar location. With his family's household bursting at the seams with product scattered everywhere, Johnny and his father renovated an old boat garage in Weymouth, Massachusetts, that became the first shop as well as company headquarters. The new space had plenty of room for all of his business needs, but Johnny wished for a location that would give him more exposure in the Boston market.

In 2006, a site for the store was chosen at 279 Newbury Street. The store was instantaneously recognized as an exclusive boutique with stores such as Chanel, Marc Jacobs, Armani, Nike Town, Gap, Burberry, Polo Ralph Lauren, Rugby, French Connection, and Cole Haan located nearby. This choice location, combined with Johnny's local reputation among young people, made the store a hit.

The Johnny Cupcakes store is designed to reflect the brand and Johnny's personality as a prankster. Instead of the traditional rolling racks, T-stands, and four-way fixtures that are common in clothing stores, the Johnny Cupcakes shop looks like a bakery. The store features a four-foot-tall dough mixer from the 1940s in the window, and bakers' racks and cases with stainless-steel trim. T-shirts are folded and placed in traditional baked goods display cases (Figure 7.3). The wooden floor, installed by Johnny's father, gives the store a touch of elegance. For atmospherics, the employees use vanilla-scented air fresheners throughout the store so it smells like a bakery, and free cupcakes are handed out whenever a new T-shirt design is released or a new collection is launched (Figure 7.4).

On opening day at the Newbury Street store, more than 600 individuals came to check it out and buy T-shirts (see Figure 7.4). In an interview with National Public Radio, Johnny dis-

FIGURE 7.3 The interior of the Johnny Cupcakes store on Newbury Street in Boston.

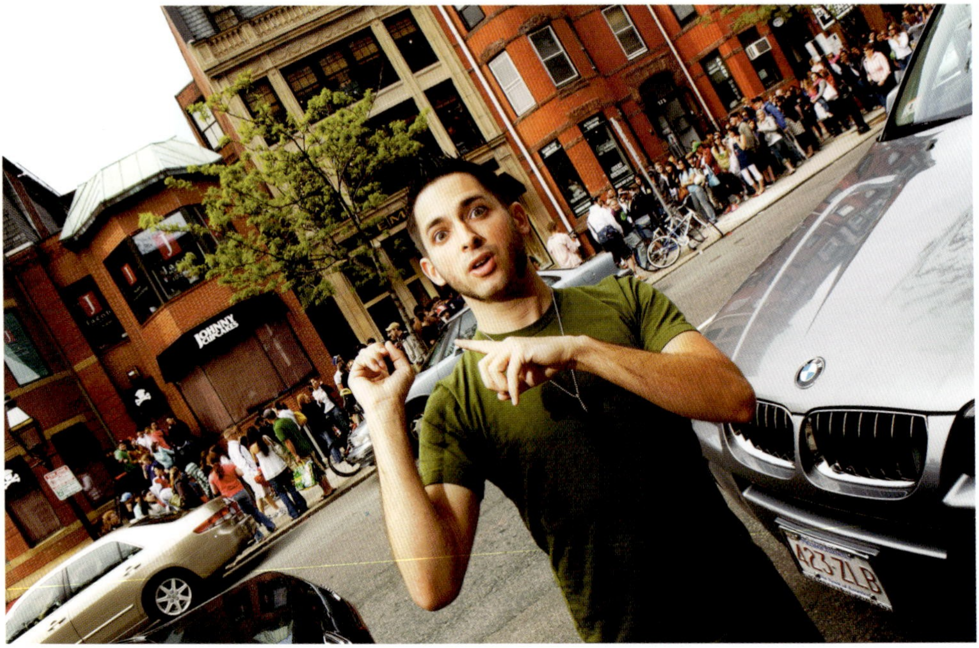

FIGURE 7.4 Johnny standing in front of his store on opening day . . . look at that line!

cussed his cult superstar status: "People will buy one of everything. And every time I'm here, people will ask to get their picture taken with me. They'll ask for my autograph. It is just word of mouth. It's unbelievable."[8] Johnny works hard to maintain the unique nature of his products as sales and demand for the T-shirts increases.

INTERVIEW
Public Relations and Branding: Talking with Jennifer Lea Cohan

Johnny Cupcakes has created an image for himself that is stylish and unique. He has created a personal brand that is easily understood by the public in person and on his website. He maintains a tremendous aura that reflects great public relations. Jennifer Lea Cohan, president of Savory Public Relations in Philadelphia, has focused on the culinary world, but her experience in public relations and degree in fashion design give

her a unique perspective on how fashion branding and publicity mix.

Why do you think a good fashionable image is important to have in the eyes of the public?
Fashionable image might be a little constricting. I think that consistency in one's image, whether fashionable or not, is important, as is determining the image that one is trying to project to one's fans. Am I a reckless pop star in skimpy attire leaving an L.A. club at 6 A.M. or am I a quirky indie actress clad in vintage clothes at the Union Square farmer's market? Also, the public also likes iconic things about their stars, whether it's Mario Battle's orange clogs or Anna Wintour's bob.

Do you think that celebrities need to have a strong personal style?
Having a strong personal style is alluring to the media, whether that style is horrific, glamorous, trendsetting, or all of the above. In the age of paparazzi, some celebrities haven't a clue about fashion, which is why the personal stylist is so dominant these days.

Do you think personal style and brand image are the same thing?
I think that personal style is an important element of a person's "brand." There is confusion [between the two terms] as they are so intertwined. I look at personal style as an ingredient; the main dish is the overall brand.

In the future, do you think fashion branding is going to become more important or less significant?
We are getting so homogenous with fashion that anything one can do to pull apart from the pack will be valuable.

How difficult is it to have a career in public relations?
It is very much about, as a brilliant writer friend of mine says, "Managing your clients' expectations." There is a lot of psychology behind PR, particularly with difficult clients. Every publicist has sat across from a client and thought, "For the love of God, you are so out of touch and self important, and your [restaurant, fashion line, project, career, or consumer product] is so underwhelming! And you want to be featured in *GQ*, on the *Today Show*, reviewed in *The New York Times*, rub shoulders with celebrities, or seen as a socially conscious captain of industry." And then you leave these meetings and get to work putting together the pieces. Many people don't realize that getting PR requires a lot of work on the part of the client, such as returning calls and e-mails, providing information quickly, revealing embarrassing details, and living up to intensified media scrutiny. But it's not all negative—making a new media connection, working on a cool project and, of course, doing PR for someone you absolutely adore is wonderful. If you really care for a client, they will be in your thoughts all the time, and you are apt to go above and beyond for them whenever possible.

When you represent a celebrity do you think that it's important for you to look a certain way? Do you have to "brand" Jennifer?
When I go somewhere with a client I am always put together, even if it is a casual gathering. A client wants someone who commands attention but does not siphon their spotlight. I have one prim and stylish client whose entire persona is clad in vintage 1960s and 1970s garments; when I am with her, I plumb my wardrobe for my own vintage pieces. Another client is a beautiful Puerto Rican chef; she is very feminine and glamorous, which inspires me in my own dress. As a brand, "Jennifer" is very grounded, and known

for her sense of humor and eclectic taste in clothing, friends, food—everything. My personal style mirrors this brand with a diverse wardrobe and low-maintenance wash'n'wear California girl hairstyle.

Maintaining and Expanding the Johnny Cupcakes Brand

Johnny the entrepreneur is remarkably savvy when it comes to maintaining competitive advantage. Each design is special to him, and he feels that exclusivity is crucial to the success of his brand. Johnny does not want the success of his company to make his products "common," with everyone wearing the same

FIGURE 7.5 Johnny has expanded his line to include handbags that retail for $250. Note the branding details such as the oven mitts hanging from the handle.

Johnny Cupcakes products. In addition to manufacturing a limited quantity of each item, the company continues to evolve by adding new products. For example, the company has added a line of handbags that retail for more than $250 (Figure 7.5).

The product line and marketing campaigns continue to reflect Johnny's passion for popular culture. Many of his T-shirt designs mimic the ideologies that are reflective of twentieth-century style and popular logo design; however, each features a special twist for the youthful customer, such as the Bon Appétit T-shirt in Figure 7.6.

To closely monitor his business, Johnny works with select wholesalers and has 12 of his close friends monitor and fill online

FIGURE 7.6 Johnny's designs reflect nostalgia and popular culture, as in this bon Bon appétit Appétit hoodie.

orders. Another team of employees runs both of his shops, and his mother still works for him trademarking designs and taking care of paperwork.

So You Want to Start Your Own Business

Many young people dream of finding success. To help people to realize their ambitions, Johnny has created a list of dos and don'ts for young entrepreneurs about viral fashion-branding techniques. These include the following:

1. *Don't Rush.* First impressions are everything. Do not release any product unless you know for sure it is as good as you can get it to be.
2. *Don't get bummed out if you go broke.* You have to spend money to make money.
3. *Travel, travel, travel.* Go and see the world, get to know other people, and learn about other cultures.
4. *Get a catchy domain name.* Do something different, original, and memorable. Take your time coming up with a name.
5. *Limit product.* Do not mass produce anything. Everyone wants what nobody has.
6. *Be prepared to toss out any relationships or hobbies.* You will have to put 110 percent into building any company. You need to get your own act together before taking on a relationship.
7. *Focus, focus!* Living a drug-free, alcohol-free lifestyle has enabled me to save money, think straight, live healthy, focus more, and use my time wisely. I am not saying do what I did. I am just pointing out that you are going to have to make your company your first priority.
8. *Personalize your online orders.* Johnny Cupcakes shirts are wrapped in special cupcake tissue paper, and usually come with a Ninja Turtles or Garbage Pail Kids card. Take a couple of

extra minutes to do what puts a gigantic smile on someone's face! You don't have to copy my method of candy, but a thank-you goes a long way with a customer.[9]

Are the Cupcakes Done Yet?

Johnny Cupcakes will never be done! The company is planning years ahead. In his own words, Johnny likes to "mix things up," with new design concepts and lines of ties, handbags, toys, silk-screened limited-edition posters, housewares, sneakers, jackets, and lots more. And a new store has opened on Melrose Avenue in Los Angeles.

Johnny and others who maximize the use of viral branding have redefined how fashion brands are promoted. It is not flashy advertising that allows retailers to become successful, but a passion for the business and a concern for customers. One of the most important Johnny Cupcakes business practices, which many retail conglomerates should be practicing, is listening to the customers. In today's competitive retail market, youth-focused companies such as Urban Outfitters and Gap are not listening to or rewarding their clients the way Johnny Cupcakes does. Johnny's company is one step ahead and not missing a beat!

Discussion Questions

1. What is viral fashion branding? How did this form of branding make Johnny Cupcakes a well-known product line in the youth market?
2. Why is viral fashion branding a good method for promoting product? Can you think of other brands that are currently using this process?
3. How does Johnny Cupcakes allow customers to feel like they are special? Is this important and why?
4. Do you think the Johnny Cupcakes brand relates to older cus-

tomers like the baby-boomers and generation Xers? Why or why not? How does his use of nostalgia and popular culture influence his ability to reach different audiences?

5. In your opinion, is Johnny Cupcakes a unique brand? What other items would you include in his product line?

Exercise

You are the new designer of a product line of fashion goods. Using Johnny Cupcakes as a model, how would you promote this product to your target market? You have a very limited advertising budget and have to do most of the work yourself, so how would you spread the word about your product? How long do you think it would take for your product to reach the national or international markets? Why?

CHAPTER EIGHT

A GREAT IDEA FROM A NEW DESIGNER

DANTE BEATRIX

It's All in the Graphics

There are few people you meet during your lifetime who make a permanent impression. For me, Dante Pauwels is one of those people. It all began when we had French class together in high school. Dante dressed impeccably and was always prepared for class. Anyone who wanted to know about the latest fashion trends turned to Dante. She was the quintessential fashion diva among her peers, and everyone envied her skill at putting outfits together. What was really cool about Dante was that if she couldn't find something to her liking, she would design and make it herself.

I knew even then that Dante would someday make a lasting impression on the world. I had an inkling it would relate to fashion, but never dreamed that she would found a company that would grow to sell products from the United States to Asia.

A Shift in Focus

Initially, the Dante Beatrix company focused on bags for every purpose: totes, laptop bags, gym bags, diaper bags, and pet carriers. Its initial mission was to create the bag that a girl with the "it" bag would use for all her other stuff. But over time it became apparent that what was really selling the bags were the graphic designs and the wonderful company logo (Figure 8.1).

Dante Beatrix decided to expand into new products, such as T-shirts and children's backpacks. The functional features of the bags were important, but the hedonic pleasure the consumer received from its branding and graphics is what drove its business. So the company changed its mission to a model similar to that of Paul Frank, a company that depends on unique signature graphics to sell its products. The market's positive response to this shift in strategy led the team at Dante Beatrix to realize the reason for its success: *It's all in the graphics!*

Why Handbags?

Sales in the handbag market have risen over 20 percent in recent years. Current sales have reached volumes of more than $6 billion, growing at a rate of about 6 to 8 percent per year and expected to continue. The consumer demand for more luxury brands is driving the market.

Research has shown that in the handbag industry, when consumers are given a choice to buy more expensive handbags over less expensive models, most will trade up to the higher price-point bags.[1] This is due to the simple fact that most women look at their handbags as an investment in their wardrobe. For many women, purse shopping has changed from just finding an adequate accessory to being almost an obsession; a guilty pleasure.

FIGURE 8.1 The Dante Beatrix logo, which resembles a halo and devil horns.

Searching for the perfect handbag is not easy in a market that is inundated with many styles, fabrications, brands, and price points.

The core age of female consumers driving sales in the handbag market is between 25 and 44. Female consumers between the ages of 18 and 24 are the second most influential group. Many of these younger shoppers buy more purses than their older counterparts; however, those between the ages of 25 and 44 have a tendency to buy higher-priced handbags.[2]

Although many women might argue that they do not purchase handbags purely for the sake of status, handbag research has shown that women do rely on the approval of their peer group when buying new bags.[3] This is due to the high visibility of these accessories in public spheres. A handbag telegraphs something about a woman's socioeconomic status and taste. In other words, women view handbags as a personal extension of themselves and their personality. A handbag represents a woman's identity, much like a briefcase may indicate a man's status or profession.

Many women will not buy a handbag when they shop alone because they need a companion or friend to give his or her approval; friends, relatives, and spouses can tell when a purse suits an individual's personal style.[4] For example, a recent interview with an informant revealed that her neighbor often asks her to go purse shopping. "The last time we went shopping my neighbor and I had this huge debate on whether or not she was a *white purse* or *red purse* kind of woman. Then after we decided on color, she had to know what handbag silhouette suited her body type. I know how important the right bag decision can be so I was patient, but this search took over two hours!"[5]

Not only are women having difficulty deciding on the correct colors and shapes of their handbags, many are conflicted about pricing. Magazines and various media publications consistently bombard their readers with handbags priced anywhere from \$500 to \$100,000. Despite the fact that magazines are constantly creating an aspirational brand image and desire for expensive bags, many women still purchase bags in the \$100 to \$150 range. Market research also reveals that all levels of working female shoppers view handbags with the same regard as wristwatches, laptop computers, and jewelry. Many women see handbags as investments, so purchasing a bag for between \$650 and \$1,500 is not perceived as a financial burden. Therefore, luxury handbags are sought after by professional women who use the bags every day instead of a briefcase or laptop computer case.[6]

Most women purchase about three handbags a year with some women only purchasing one or two. However, the number of units sold per year is showing signs of slowing, primarily owing to the fact that most women are trading up, buying fewer bags at higher prices. But even though fewer units are being sold, the dollar volume is still increasing. The average amount that a woman spends on handbags annually is about \$143. Also, it is interesting to note that most women will increase their handbag budget if they spy the perfect bag.[7] In other words, women will charge or take out credit to buy the perfect handbag. Money becomes less of an issue when a woman has a strong attachment to a bag.

Black, Hispanic, and Asian women seem more concerned about matching their handbags to their outfits and shoes. These women are more brand and style conscious than their white counterparts, who will use an all-in-one bag for every event. Moreover, research has shown that black women are more likely to buy designer knockoffs from street vendors or to attend purse parties where they are sold. This fashionable group is brand conscious and price savvy. To some of these women, getting a bargain is the key to being stylish—only a fool pays retail. Many black women avidly follow handbag trends to the extreme, are usually fashion leaders in this category, and are more stylish. They do not adhere to social peer pressure from others, and take more risks with fashion and accessories; buying fakes allows for a designer look without the price.[8]

Pet Carriers, Baby Bags, and Backpacks

Besides trendy and luxury handbags, other bag categories impact the lives of female shoppers. These include diaper bags, totes, laptop cases, children's bags, and pet carriers. Although many of us will never require the use of a diaper bag, some, like me, may use a pet carrier or buy a laptop bag. This great diversity of bag types has led to the growth in this product category.

Pet carriers are currently all the rage in major metropolitan areas around the globe. Once used primarily for transporting pets during air travel, now these hip carriers have become like handbags. A recent article in *TimeOut New York* titled "Pet Mania . . . Unleashed," stated that New Yorkers were spending thousands of dollars on their pets and accessories.[9]

In 2002, the American Pet Products Manufacturers Association declared that over 64 million households had pets. That number continues to grow and is not expected to slow down in major cities like New York where over 1.7 million dogs and 1.9 million cats currently live. Between the years of 1994 and 2007 the amount of money spent on household pets went from $17 to more than $36 billion.[10]

Many pet owners consider their pets to be their children and indulge in the same methods that parents use to spoil their kids. There are doggy daycare centers, grooming salons, pet hospitals, and fashion pet boutiques. These trends reflect current ideology and challenge the ideas of what makes a family. There is a growing trend among single professionals who do not want to have children; they opt to adopt a dog instead, and same-sex couples often adopt pets rather than children.[11] There is no escaping the fact that pets have become an important part of current families, but the growth in pet products has not yet surpassed consumer demands for durable baby products.

Currently, sales of child-related durable products like diaper bags and backpacks are growing at a rate of 1 to 4 percent per year.[12] The increased growth in these products is due in part to the modern mother who wants her own sense of fashion reflected in her baby bag. Current mothers want a bag that is both stylish and multifunctional, and active mothers want diaper bags that connect to jogging strollers and are designed from robust fabrics that will hold up to heavy use.

But where do women go to find bags that are both stylish and fashionable? In a recent survey conducted by the Mintel Report, over 60 percent of respondents stated that they conduct Internet searches for the perfect bag prior to even visiting a brick-and-mortar retailer. Most stated that they find more unique and stylish products from individual online retailers than at big-box stores such as Target, Wal-Mart, or the local baby products superstore.[13]

The children's backpack area continues to flourish through strategies with licensing agencies such as sports teams, television networks, and iconic characters from conglomerates like Disney. Children still want backpacks that are colorful and include exciting themes that relate to the latest cartoon or iconic image. This is similar to their parents' generation, who coveted lunchboxes with branded themes such as Barbie, The Brady Bunch, pop music groups, and celebrities.

INTERVIEW

Trend Forecasting, Fashion Branding, and Life Lessons: Talking with Jill Walker-Roberts

Sometimes fashion trends do not begin with clothing. They can start with accessories and work their way into wardrobes.

Companies such as Dante Beatrix need to be on the cutting edge of fashion. Often they rely on trend forecasters for advice. Jill Walker-Roberts is the president of Walker-Roberts Consulting, a trend-forecasting company. She has had an extensive career in retail—from salesperson to top fashion executive. Her passion for trend forecasting and brand creation has allowed her to travel all over the world.

How did your experiences in the fashion industry lead to your current success in trend forecasting?

I have been working in the fashion industry since 1981. I started as a salesperson in Casual Corner in Water Tower Place in Chicago. . . . [T]here was a store on the top floor of the building that looked like a disco, sounded like a concert, and felt like a club. Most of my lunch hours were spent going upstairs and observing this phenomenon. I even got to be on a first-name basis with the manager, who told me the store was only one of five in the United States. The name of the store was The Limited Express. [I eventually became] an assistant buyer in the corporate offices at Limited Express in Columbus, Ohio.

After I left Express, I landed a job at Paul Harris in Indianapolis as a buyer [and then moved to] the Brown Group in Clayton, Missouri. The [next] change was to move to New York and get a job and, a month later, get married. It is challenging to find a job in New York if you say you're a Midwesterner. The saving grace was The Limited. It has opened doors unlike any other experience. I landed a job in product development. Then, I was promoted to source factories in Mexico and Central America. . . . [A]fter about two years, I started looking [again]. Eventually, I began to use my skills as a colorist, a sample shopper, and predictor of future key items to start my own company. I began by servicing existing clients. It evolved into doing trend boards and reports for Asian makers in Shanghai and Hong Kong for both home decor and garments, and finally, working to establish new clients and maintaining those listed.

Why is trend forecasting so important and how has is it changing?

It is a predictor of what will be. . . . It not only determines clothing, but the appliance, home decor, food, electronics, and automobile industries. I believe retailers have changed. H&M and Zara and Ikea are rocking the world with their runway-to-floor knockoffs, in 3- to 6-week lead-times. The home decor market is one year ahead of the apparel market on trend. Look at the prints in Ikea; they will be next year's dress print. Today, unfortunately, we live in a climate of revisiting old trend stories. Some say this is "vintage." I challenge designers to think outside of the box. It has been a long time since we have seen a "new" style.

How does a company search for trends?

Different markets seek out trend inspiration in various geographical places. Many contemporary designers search the boutiques of San Tropez, London, Hong Kong, or Amsterdam for small designers to emulate and also get an overall vibe on silhouette and style. Swimwear and activewear folks are always looking at Hawaii, Brazil, South Beach, San Moritz, and any "next" location. Extreme sports venues are a popular observation area. For mass appeal, department stores, big box stores, and specialty retailers use the following: the Big 3 for spring style inspiration have always been Miami, San Tropez, and L.A. The Big 3 for fall/winter style inspiration have always been Montreal, London, and Paris, with Amsterdam added for denim makers.

There are also specialized venues, like the Pitti Filatti in Florence, a yarn show that many sweater makers attend; Premiere Vision, Paris, where many colorists and trend directors go to observe; Interstoff in Asia is also a big fabric venue. Luxury brands are very sought after in Asia and can be observed there as well, but oftentimes the garment pattern is made for an Asian consumer. The runway shows in Paris and Bryant Park, New York, are huge with buyers and fashion directors, celebrities, and media. But overall most buyers and trend offices do not attend them because they have very few available seats. I have heard that Tommy (Hilfiger) and Ralph (Lauren) and others still like to observe urban street fashion for inspiration. I find that to be great in London, Vancouver, Chicago, and L.A. There are up-and-coming places that will be an inspiration like Dubai, Dubrovnik, Istanbul, Shanghai, and Moscow. Brazil is extremely body conscious and has its own style. I personally think film, bar and club decor, luxury hotel architecture and design, television and travel destinations affect trends greatly. Also politics impacts the trends. Example: Have you ever seen so many shades of gray in automobiles? This is a direct result of people's mood, the economy and politics—murky, gloomy, undistinguishable, solemn, and depressed.

How has fashion branding impacted the area of trend forecasting? And is branding here to stay?

It is all logo overkill and about the consumer remembering it, like a breakfast cereal. Target, Louis Vuitton, Victorinox, Old Navy, DKNY, all have immediate image recognition. I see it (branding) as a marketing scheme that won't stop. I believe the consumer feels oversaturated, like monograms in the late 1970s. They may need a visual break, or a moment to breathe. There will be a company that stands up and says "we are the anti-branding" company. Think about it . . . an all white background with a pin dot in the center. No words. You would remember this just the same as a font, a bold color, or a jingle.

What is your advice to any student who wants to pursue the area of trend forecasting as a career? What sort of experience should they have?

Start by apprenticing or interning with a mentor. Know the trend publications; SnapFashun, Milou Ket, Trendzine, Peclers Paris, Promostyl, and Le Book are a few to investigate. Look at seasonal color predictions. Know how to approve colors. Pay particular attention to accessories, both luxury and novelty; this is usually an early predictor of a trend that will evolve, especially color. People feel more confident buying a necklace, handbag, or shoe in a wild pattern or totally innovative look, than a pair of pants or jacket. The uses of optic brights in accessories are a good example of this for Spring 2008. You may want to look at www.apparelsearch.com and click on the fashion forecasting or trend analyst sections for more trend and color office information. Read the trades like *Women's Wear Daily*, read international papers, and magazines, go to movies, walk the streets, and observe. Analyze trends as you go through your day.

The History of Dante Beatrix

Dante Pauwels completed her master's degree in product design at Stanford University and then briefly manufactured her own collection of housewares. These home accessories were called Pop-Up, two pieces of which are in the permanent collection of the San Francisco Museum of Modern Art. Pauwels then worked for the Martha Stewart catalogue, where she helped to design a ubiquitous rubber tote bag. She had always planned to start her own business; so with years of experience in graphic design, advertising, and product design, she began Dante Beatrix.

While living in New York City, Pauwels noticed many women had too much stuff to carry at once. She saw women toting around two or three bags just to accommodate all their belongings. Many times the bags were unattractive or really did not seem to fit the style of the woman carrying them. Her company's website Dante Beatrix stated it best: "Everyday life is full of loads and loads of stuff. So much stuff, in fact, that finding an elegant way to carry it all can be a real challenge."[14]

> How is a starlet going to get all of her makeup and clothing from the car to the Green Room?
>
> How is a mum going to walk down the street and look completely cool and chic while carrying five diapers and a sippy cup? And could pops take mum's bag for a moment and maintain his manhood?
>
> How is a Miss Achiever going to get her laptop to the meeting without looking like an Amway sales rep?
>
> How is Trixie, the sweetest little doggy in the world, going to travel with dignity when it's time for a checkup?
>
> These are the problems that fascinate us at Dante Beatrix.
>
> There is no end of talent devoted to creating the next "it" handbag, but what about all those other bags that get you through the day?
>
> We don't think that you should compromise on fashion when it comes to navigating the everyday world.
>
> We make bags that are functional, beautifully tailored, timeless and simple enough to compliment a woman's personal style. Maybe you're being photographed by paparazzi, or maybe the only people who'll scrutinize your

outfit today are the six-year-olds in the carpool, but we want you to get on with your busy day in style.[15]

Pauwels launched Dante Beatrix in 2004. Realizing she didn't want to compete in the overly saturated handbag market, Pauwels made it her mission to create a secondary bag for toting around extra personal items. She started by making functional colorful totes, and customers started asking her to design a diaper bag. Dante's first diaper bag included a roll-up changing mat for baby. The bag was very sophisticated and stylish (Figure 8.2). But expectant moms were not the only ones who desired Dante Beatrix diaper bags; various women began to buy them for daily hauling. "I guess there was just a need for a big, utilitarian bag out there and no one had anything," stated Pauwels in a 2004 interview with *WWD Accessories*.[16]

The success of the bags was due to their design, price, and colors. Also, when she first entered the bag market, no one was designing fashionable baby bags for women, and many tote bags were either in basic colors or more utilitarian than fashionable. Pauwels found success through designing bags in fun colors that

FIGURE 8.2 A gray-and-khaki baby tote with changing mat.

could be used as baby bags or as regular totes. She wanted all of her bags, regardless of their use, to give women a fashionable look. Another key ingredient for her success was the very reasonable price point of her products. Her earlier totes retailed from $140 to $198; in the company's second year Dante Beatrix garnered over $300,000 in wholesale sales. Even though Pauwels had never sought to enter the baby market, it was where her customers led her.

The Business Fattens

Her initial success gave Pauwels the confidence to design other types of bags. So she expanded into other products to include more styles of baby bags, cosmetics bags, regular totes, computer bags, and pet carriers. She wanted to design secondary bags for every need in a woman's life: baby, gym, work, pets, and so on. After a year of pursuing this strategy, Pauwels found that her company was no longer growing at an accelerated rate. She analyzed her business and received advice from colleagues. She then decided that her strategy to design secondary bags for every need in a woman's life was too ambitious for a company of her size. She found that each new style of bag she created involved finding a different store buyer and potentially attending another trade show. She looked at her competitors and discovered that they focused on a single category. A pet carrier company could design new bags and show them to store buyers with whom it had established relationships. Each new product could be fed to this same buyer. Pauwels's strategy, however, meant that she had to track down numerous buyers and stores. Building so many relationships would be difficult and diluted the brand. Pauwels decided to focus on her strength—baby bags (Figure 8.3).

Around this time, Pauwels had two friends who wanted to join her as partners. In 2006, Claire Theobald joined Dante Beat-

FIGURE 8.3 An orange "bébé" stroller tote.

rix. Claire is an overachiever who graduated with degrees from Yale in architecture and graphic design. Before working in the retail market, Claire designed museum exhibits and branded environments for Ralph Applebaum Associates in New York. She met Pauwels when they worked briefly together in a branding group of Ogilvy and Matheson. Then Marcus Woolcott joined Dante Beatrix. He and Pauwels had been friends since they worked together at an advertising agency after college. He worked for several leading agencies and consultancies, and was awarded the Cannes Lion (a distinguished advertising award).

The Future Is Branding

Like many entrepreneurs, Pauwels, Theobald, and Woolcott continually examine their business strategy. Analysis of the sales of their baby bags led to a pivotal discovery: although their customers love their bags, what they really like about Dante Beatrix products are the graphics! Upon realizing this, the team quickly designed new products to capitalize on this finding. This time, they designed products that would sell to their existing group of buyers. They introduced new products, such as children's backpacks and graphically fashionable totes (Figures 8.4 and 8.5). The company maintains its competitive edge by pricing its bags at a reasonable market value with children's backpacks ranging from $36 to $55 and women's totes from $110 to $220.

Dante Beatrix plans to branch into other fashion areas such as children's T-shirts and sweaters. The company plans to evolve from primarily a bag company into a limited-line, specialty retail company similar to Paul Frank Industries.

With the reinvention of the company, Pauwels started to focus on specific trade shows. At one particular show, the Asian market noticed her company and Dante Beatrix became a hit in the Japanese marketplace. Her new stroller bags with their bright colors and fun themes (see Figure 8.3) were popular among Asian women. "I was so surprised by the success of the

FIGURE 8.4 A little kids backpack with kid-friendly lion graphic.

FIGURE 8.5 A "haul" tote big enough to carry pretty much everything with a fun beetle design.

bags in the Asian market," said Pauwels. "Our customers in Japan love the colors and the graphics."[17]

Reflecting the current trends among women, this company is successful because the product line is unique and stylish. Additionally, Dante Beatrix sells many of its bags at retailers such as Nordstrom, Barneys New York, A Pea in the Pod, and Babystyle. Some bags are sold on the Internet, which has helped to expand the brand to obscure markets and areas where there are few retail outlets. Currently, online offerings are found at Zappos.com and, of course, at DanteBeatrix.com. By utilizing both brick-and-mortar retailers and the Internet, Dante Beatrix reaches both domestic and international markets.

Pauwels believes that the primary reason Dante Beatrix has maintained its competitive edge is due to its willingness to evolve with the marketplace; first regular totes, next baby totes, then totes for every need, back to baby totes, and finally graphics. Dante Pauwels is proud of the company she has created and although I cannot see into the future, I can tell you that Dante Beatrix is worth watching as the company captures the fashion market by listening to its customers—one at a time.

Discussion Questions

1. Why do consumers feel such a close attachment to their bags?
2. What is your favorite brand of bag, briefcase, or backpack, and why? How does this brand reflect your personality? Do you think you will ever switch to a different brand?
3. Now that you have read this chapter, go to www.dantebeatrix.com and explain how the company has evolved. What is the latest news? How do you think the line reflects current fashion?
4. Why do you think Dante Beatrix is so successful with the company's ideas to pursue graphic design instead of just focusing on bag design? Is branding the key element that drives you to purchase a bag, briefcase, or backpack? Look at a bag you have now. Is it designer? What is the brand? What features *really* make it special, or is it really just the name that makes it unique? Describe your answers in detail.

Exercise

Many of us have an idea for a branded fashion product that is missing in the world. Design and brand a fashion product that you think is missing from the marketplace. Before you start you will need to conduct research to see if it already exists. Also, you should figure out if there is a need for the product. Use current periodicals such as *Women's Wear Daily* or *WWD Accessories* to help you with your research. Explain your findings to the class.

3
2

CHAPTER NINE

CREATING A TELEVISION BRAND

BRINI MAXWELL

Now Why Didn't You Think of That?

In 1998 a young actor named Ben Sander became Brini Maxwell. With the help of his theatrical parents, the idea for Sander to play Brini was inspired and developed, in part, by a collection of retro-styled home fashions, cookbooks, and magazines. Earlier television personalities, such as Sue Ann Nivens and Mary Richards from the *The Mary Tyler Moore Show* and Ann Marie from *That Girl,* stimulated the brand vision of Maxwell's domestic *divaness* that Sander and his family sought to emulate. An icon was born that rivaled the glories of past celebrity homemakers; a modern "woman" with a flair for budget, mid-twentieth-century modern style, and an approach to the domestic arts that made you forget that *she* is a *he.*

With each broadcast of her show, Brini Maxwell demonstrates a new recipe, home repair, fashion segment, or interview. In the process, she creates a brand that is distinctly hers. Her reinvention of a bygone era pays homage to her predecessors while maintaining a contemporary sensibility, and exceeds the creative efforts of her current competition. Brini has accomplished this by creating a unique *visual milieu. Milieu* is a French term that means an individual's physical or social environment. The phrase *visual milieu* refers to what is observed when viewing milieu. Brini Maxwell's visual milieu is composed of retro twentieth-century modern and contemporary designs that were popular from the 1950s until the 1970s. Brini Maxwell wears vintage fashions from these time periods and emulates the lifestyle of these past decades to create her visual milieu. Maxwell's sense of twentieth-century retro style, her use of camp, and mannerisms reminiscent of historical times, are also incorporated into the show's setting, production values, and the themes of each show. These elements collectively are what I refer to as *Maxwell's visual milieu* (Figure 9.1).

The story of Brini Maxwell is unique. Sander became a na-

FIGURE 9.1 Brini on the phone in her Los Angeles home.

tional celebrity by taking a simple idea from his own personal collection of vintage products to create a fashion-branded style. Maxwell's adventure reveals that through the magic of television and the ability to develop a targeted brand, success can blossom to the point of iconic stardom.

Ben Sander, Brini Maxell, and the Show

Ben Sander was born and raised in New York and also lived in Ohio and Kansas City. After graduating from high school, he attended the Fashion Institute of Technology in New York City where he studied fashion design. After college, Ben Sander worked in the New York City garment industry where he felt that his personal style was stunted by corporate structure. This led Sander to search for other creative avenues.

The idea for the Maxwell visual milieu came about when Ben Sander purchased a set of Pyrex bowls for $15 at a Salvation Army store. Feeling it was a shame that no one would ever see the remarkable household objects that were used for food preparation, he became despondent for days, moping around his Chelsea apartment. Then he had an idea! He would create a cooking show. With the help of his parents, actress Mary Jane Wells and theater professor Peter Sander, they designed a show that featured cooking segments and general household tips. The idea and branding philosophy was simple: "What we wanted to show is that *gracious* is a state of mind. It is not what you own or where you live. It is how you treat other people and how you care about your environment."[1]

The Sander family funded the show entirely. They established V.R.U.S.P. Productions, and Sander's mother produced the program while his father directed it. Brini Maxwell began in 1998 as *At Home with Tigs*, which focused on a contemporary jet-setter known as Tigs Vanderveer; however, Sander soon realized that the Vanderveer character was too stuffy. Sander decided on the name Brini, which was modeled after Stephanie Powers's character Sabrina from the 1985 miniseries *Deceptions*. The name *Maxwell* was derived from Barbara Streisand's character Judy Maxwell in the hit comedy film *What's Up, Doc?*

Sander's collection of cookbooks, magazines, furnishings, and other mid-century delights would be used in every episode. For the show's location, Sander turned to his apartment in the Chelsea section of Manhattan. The entire show—cooking, entertaining, interviews with celebrities, and home renovations—was produced in a teeny, fourth-floor, 600-square-foot, walk-up apartment!

But the lack of space did not mean a lack of style. To create the perfect look, Sander turned to his expertise in design and garment sewing. The Maxwell visual milieu included fashions reminiscent of the 1950s, 1960s, and early 1970s. To create a believable retro look required both skill and research. Sander was born in 1969, so many of Brini's outfits were not like those that he had grown up with as a young television fan. Sander viewed episodes of *That Girl*, *Mary Tyler Moore*, *Donna Reed*, and Rosalind Russell in *Auntie Mame* for inspiration. Brini Maxwell became the character that Ben Sander was not. He hid behind her to reach out to audiences. Brini Maxwell was the iconic branded symbol, while the androgynous voice of Ben Sander reflected his knowledge of retro fashion, style, cooking, home improvement, and everything he knew that related to home advice.

The show was an instant success among New Yorkers, who anxiously waited for each episode. Sanders created a Lucy and Ethel relationship between Brini Maxwell and her sidekick, Mary Ellen. Unlike Maxwell, Mary Ellen was not a homemaker, was not very ladylike, and wore modern, contemporary apparel. The relationship between the two made the show more popular than ever! The show featured celebrities like comedian Margaret Cho who demonstrated how to make fondue with chocolate, pound cake, strawberries, and pineapples.

On Saturday, January 8, 2000, Brini Maxwell was featured as "Part Martha Stewart, Part RuPaul" in *The New York Times*.[2] The article by Chris Hedges reported that New Yorkers enjoyed the show and found it provided useful advice for basic living. The report added that some Brini Maxwell fans did not *really* understand that Maxwell was a he. One fan stated, "My husband and I always enjoy your show and try to watch it every week. I must admit though that after one of your episodes I feel quite inadequate as my role of wife, and know that my hubby probably feels a twinge of regret at marrying a modern career woman instead of an efficient, elegant nest builder like you."[3]

Describing the inner workings behind his character, Sander said, "I am a *mactress*, a man who plays a female role on a television show; not a drag queen."[4] He has suggested that he does not feel comfortable in the public eye as himself; Maxwell is an alter ego of sorts. Sander describes himself as a shy, disparate person who has a hard time getting to know people. Maxwell is the opposite; she is able to adjust to any setting with any group of people.[5] Brini Maxwell, not Sander, is the brand and key spokesperson for V.R.U.S.P. Productions.

INTERVIEW

Creating a Brand Image from Scratch: Talking with Brini Maxwell

Brini Maxwell, media star, domestic goddess, and spokesmodel for Felix Populi, is a national star and has been featured on the Style Network. She is currently traveling around the globe searching for the latest in retro brands.

Why you think you have become such a media icon?
I think I represent a certain type of woman that strikes a chord with people of a certain age because they remember women like me from when they were children—their mother, an aunt, or a teacher that had a distinct sense of style, a flair for decorating, and a knack for entertaining.

Why do you think people are able to relate to your brand image?
Branding is a powerful form of communication. Putting yourself out there as a brand (and anyone can do it with a little thought and a few basic graphic design skills) can create a rapport with like-minded individuals. Luckily, what I want to communicate seems to be what people want to hear and see.

Who is your target market and why?
My target market is primarily young and urban. There is also a little crossover into forward (or nostalgic) baby boomers. Our brand is an alternative to more traditional aesthetics. It's for people who define themselves as somehow different from the norm. This is, when you think about it, a form of rebellion, which is generally a young phenomenon. Cities are the destination for making your own mark, which is what these young people want to do, ergo, our target market is young urbanites. The boomers find my brand appealing for a different reason. They see the nostalgia of what I do and find it comforting.

Do you consider yourself in competition with anyone, for example Martha Stewart? Or are you setting your own trends?
Well, I suppose in a broad sense I'm in competition with Martha Stewart, however I don't believe we are competing for viewers. I think that a lot of my viewers wouldn't watch a domestic service show if I wasn't the entertainment.

Tell us about your new line of products. Why are you focusing on home fashions instead of the clothing business?
My new product line is a small but growing collection of items for the home, including pillows, accessories for the kitchen, and soon to include crafting kits. I decided to focus on home goods because clothing is a very complicated business to start, primarily because of fit. Items must be fitted to an ideal body of some kind—your fit model—and then graded up and down to include all sizes. This means that each item you design must be made in all those sizes—a daunting proposition for manufacturing. Home goods are designed and manufactured in one size, and the patterns and construction techniques are usually much simpler.

What advice do you have for those who might want to consider starting their own business?
The more you know the better off you'll be. Do research, work in the industry you want to launch your business in, find some mentors to ask for help from. It will help you immeasurably when working up your business plan and looking for funding.

What can we expect from you in the future? And where can fans go to see or hear you?
You can expect to see a further development of the new product line at Felix Populi (www.felixpopuli.com) and you can expect to see the products at stores across the country. You can always find me on my podcasts. Just go to www.brinimaxwell.com for more information.

The Brini Maxwell Show on the Style Network

Brini's original show aired from 1998 until 2003. During those five years, the show gained a huge cult following. Producer Amy

FIGURE 9.2 Brini in her Los Angeles kitchen modeling her signature collection of domestic goods for Felix Populi.

Briamonte heard about Brini Maxwell from a friend. Briamonte watched the show and loved it. She felt the show was surreal, yet somehow comforting. She knew that viewers of the E! Network's style channel would love it, so she immediately pitched the show to the station executives.[6]

In 2004, *The Brini Maxwell Show* aired on national television, and the press went wild. On January 16, 2004, Brini Maxwell was featured front and center in *USA Today's* lifestyle section in "At Home: Brini Maxwell, TV's New Retro Matron."[7] Her new national look was more polished and sophisticated than the earlier Brini Maxwell. Pictured with sophistication, Brini Maxwell had reached national exposure (Figure 9.2).

Brini would be featured in other publications including *Entertainment Weekly*, *The Philadelphia Inquirer*, *The Advocate*, *Los Ange-*

les Times, *New York* magazine, and *Bon Appétit*. Mass coverage of the domestic diva exploded with such frenzy that Brini Maxwell found her life in a complete whirl.

The E! Network would reformat the old Brini Maxwell in a more structured and well-produced show called *The Brini Maxwell Show*. Each segment would feature specific segments to fill the 30-minute time slot. Like all of Maxwell's previous episodes, the new set was a mid-twentieth-century New York loft apartment. However, the new setting made it appear that Maxwell had moved uptown to a more stylish, uptown location. The Maxwell visual milieu had received an upgrade and the brand message was clear, concise, and definitively 1950s chic.

The new cinematography of *The Brini Maxwell Show* reflected a similar style to that of *Mister Rogers' Neighborhood* on the Public Broadcast System. The idea behind it was to make Brini Maxwell appear less threatening and more like a *natural* woman. The Style Network thought that some viewers might not find a transgendered home advice-giver comforting, so the network executives cast the show without referring to Ben Sander at all. Brini Maxwell was cast as the only star of *The Brini Maxwell Show*, not Ben Sander.

The show was divided into mini segments that offered advice on every area of the home (Table 9.1). The seven segments of each episode were each dedicated to a specific area. Table 9.1 shows the names of the segments and what each one entailed.

Brini Maxwell assumed various archetypes and styles, giving the viewer advice on every area of the home. For example, "Make Yourself at Home," "Putting It Together," "Design for Living," and "Why Didn't You Think of That?" allowed Maxwell to assume the role of a Sue Ann Nivens, Heloise, or a Martha Stewart type. The segments "Out and About," "Anywho," and "Help Me Brini!" permitted her to parody characters such as Ann Landers, Dear Abby, Oprah Winfrey, Barbara Walters, and a female version of Fred Rogers of *Mister Rogers' Neighborhood*. Major

Table 9.1. Segments of *The Brini Maxwell Show*

NAME OF SEGMENT	AREA OF HOME/LIFESTYLE
Make Yourself at Home	Minor home improvements/ comfort lifestyle/cooking
Now Why Didn't You Think of That?	New and unique ideas
Putting It Together	How to make new things/arts and crafts/cooking
Design for Living	Interior design/major home changes
Out and About	Tours of interesting and unique places
Anywho	Interviews with celebrities and friends
Help Me Brini!	Brini gives advice from letters received

celebrities appeared on the show, such as Kim Catrell from *Sex and the City*, and the former editor of *Cosmopolitan* magazine Helen Gurley Brown. Brini Maxwell was interviewed on shows such as *The Tyra Banks Show* and *Late Night with Conan O'Brien.*

The most interesting appeal of *The Brini Maxwell Show* was that it was the first time on national television that a woman who was really a man was giving advice on every area of the home. Unlike other male hosts of domestic programs such as Christopher Lowell, who only does interior design, or *Cooking with Emeril* and even *Queer Eye for the Straight Guy*, Brini Maxwell's show instructed viewers on fashion, manners, decorating, entertaining, cooking, and home repair. Like her female predecessors, Brini Maxwell was a full-service domestic diva, with one small difference: she was a he.

Beyond *The Brini Maxwell Show*

Brini's next venture was into book publishing. Her book, *Brini Maxwell's Guide to Gracious Living*, was published in 2005. The E!

Network also released the first season of her show on DVD that year, and brinimaxwell.com was launched. Next came major public appearances across the nation, at book signings, in cooking demonstrations at upscale grocery stores, and department store appearances to endorse various products. Brini Maxwell found herself traveling to conventions, speaking at universities, and making live jazz musical performances at nightclubs in Manhattan. Brini Maxwell was on national television and the Internet—the brand had become multichannel.

In late 2005 Ben Sander received bad news. The E! Network had changed management. The new president of the network had decided to cancel all shows connected to the production team that handled *The Brini Maxwell Show*. They would be allowed a second season, but after that it was over. Even though the show was among the top-rated shows on the network, the new management team did not feel it reflected their new direction.

Ben Sander did not give up. He knew Brini Maxwell had a large fan base that needed to maintain contact with their domestic diva. He researched new strategies. After he finished the last season of the show, National Public Radio agreed to produce and record the show as a one of its weekly podcasts. The podcast was instantly successful and continues to remain in the top third requested shows on iTunes. Sander began to reproduce the original show on the website, where the show continues to be broadcast. The new vidcast show has been a big hit and is viewed extensively across the nation by a new audience. Sander also created a listserv for fans to get weekly e-mail from Maxwell herself. The e-mail provides updates on Brini Maxwell endeavors and appearances.

Reinventing Ben Sander and Brini Maxwell—Felix Populi

Ben Sander knew he would need to continue the Maxwell visual milieu, but realized that it needed to be revisited. Whereas Brini

Maxwell could appear on national television on other stations, Ben Sander knew his brand had to move forward and not backward. So in 2007 he decided to release a new line of home fashions under the name of Felix Populi. The new brand name is Latin for *happy people*. The brand is a hybrid media-retail company, with Brini Maxwell as the spokesperson.

Maintaining Brini Maxwell's theme of gracious living, Felix Populi is currently researching home products such as pillows, throws, totes, sheets, towels, and draperies. The hard goods lines will consist of glassware, dishes, ceramic and wood products, plastic accent pieces, lighting, and furniture. The brand intends to also include a line of Brini Maxwell-inspired products and entertainment packages, such as "Brini Maxwell's Party in a Box." This innovative product will contain invitations, recipe cards, coasters, decorations, wine charms, and various other party supplies for throwing a festive event. Currently, the Felix Populi line is sold in upscale boutiques in Manhattan, but Ben Sander also plans to promote the line in the national market.

This new direction for the Maxwell visual milieu will generate a new public awareness for mid-twentieth-century design and style. Whatever happens, Brini Maxwell will endure in the hearts and souls of her fans who have grown and learned to live more graciously because of her kind words of confidence, creativity, and consideration.

Discussion Questions

1. What makes the Brini Maxwell television personality unique? How does her personality benefit the brand?
2. What were the steps taken by Ben Sander to develop his character, Brini Maxwell? Was he successful? Why or why not?
3. Why do you think Brini Maxwell made it into the national spotlight on television? What was her brand's message?
4. What do you think Brini Maxwell's target market is today?

Why would baby boomers be drawn to watching Brini Maxwell?

5. Why were the iTunes podcast and the reproduction of her old shows as vidcast a smart step toward rebranding Brini Maxwell? Would you have done anything differently?

Exercise

Ben Sander branded himself as Brini Maxwell. How would you create your own personal brand? What would your logo be? How would you design business cards? What would your theme song be? What would you sell? And who would your target audience be? Finally, where would you show your brand? On television, in a store, or on the Internet? Write and design a project that reflects the ideas of developing your own personal brand. Use the previous questions as an outline.

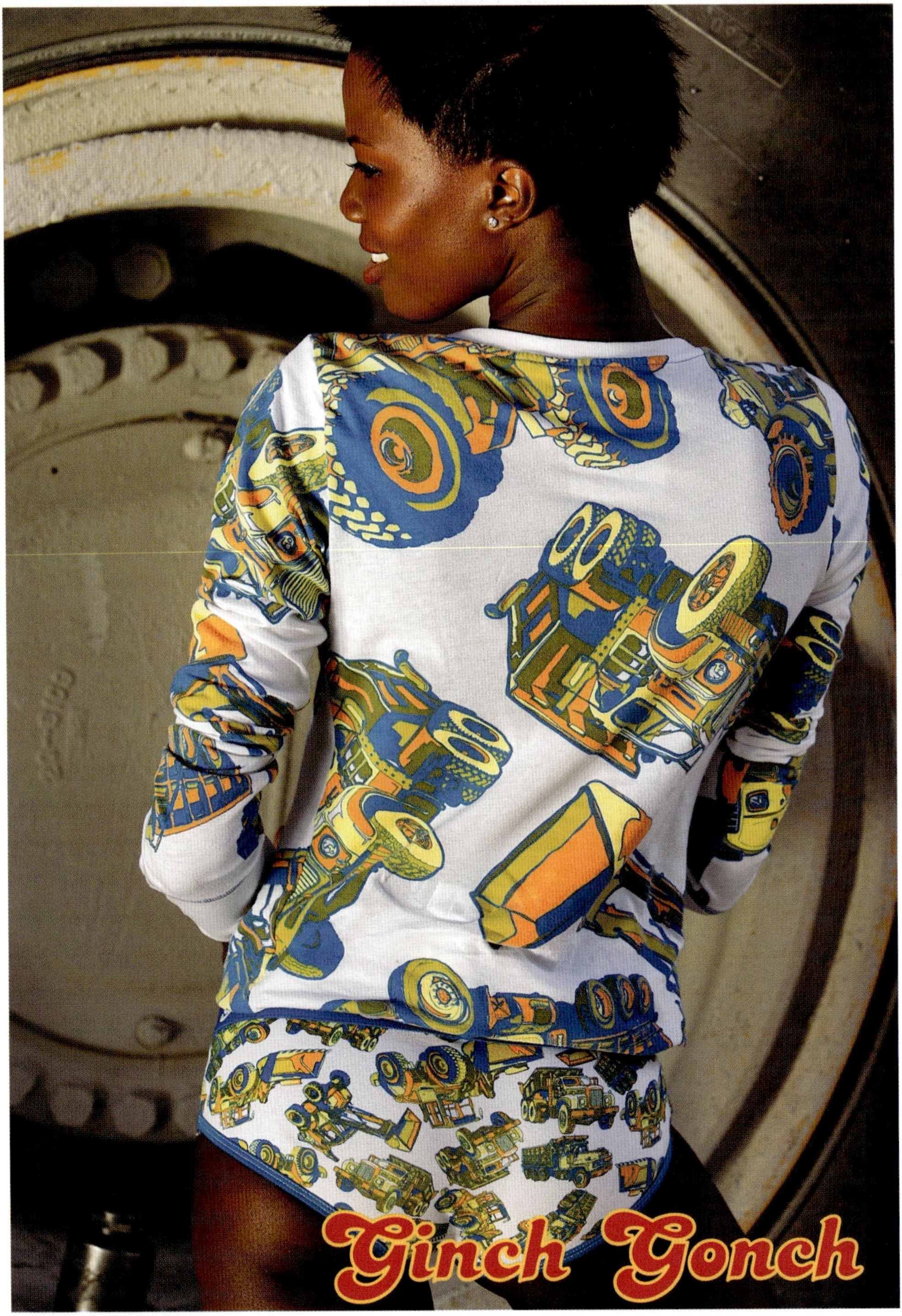
Ginch Gonch

CHAPTER TEN

NICHE FASHION BRANDING

GINCH GONCH

Live Like a Kid

The underwear market is one of the most heavily promoted product categories in fashion. With a strong advertising presence from companies such as Victoria's Secret, Calvin Klein, Hanes, and Fruit of the Loom, why would any other company try to compete? And if it did, how would it survive and be successful among consumers across the globe? Well, Ginch Gonch is doing just that.

Under the direction of its founder, Jason Sutherland, this small Vancouver-based company is moving men and women's underwear in a whole new direction, and everyone is taking notice. The company has generated such a media stir that fashion gurus everywhere are buzzing ecstatically over the garments. For example, the West Coast style editor of *People* magazine, Stephen Cojocaru, noted that Ginch Gonch underwear is a must-have for everyone's closet. This young company is selling over 200,000 units of underwear per week including briefs, jock-straps, thongs, matching T-shirts, and tanks.[1] Through the use of sexually risqué branding techniques aimed at diverse lifestyles, unique styles, and the company motto "Live Like A

Kid," Ginch Gonch demonstrates that if you have a premium product, great advertising, a market niche, and a passion for innovative branding, sales will follow.

The current trend in fashion to offer premium products at higher prices means that consumers expect each garment to be somewhat unique and special to justify the cost. Therefore, premium mass fashion garments are produced using higher quality fabrics, finishes, and designs. An example would be the luxury premium denim that currently sells for hundreds of dollars at retailers across the globe. In February 2006, the Mintel Report on denim jeans found that sales of premium denim at more than $75 a pair had grown from $600 million to over $1.1 billion.[2] These figures indicate that a market for better-quality products and premium prices exists. In keeping with the times, Ginch Gonch offers their customers a premium product.

The slowest-moving market sector in the premium denim jeans area has been men,[3] but the sector has moved faster than others in areas such as underwear. This has caused underwear manufacturers to produce premium lines and more new products for men. Many well-known luxury brands, such as Armani, have already recognized this target market. Armani now produces underwear for their mass retail outlet Armani Exchange as well as for their higher premium venue, the Emporio Armani division for whom David Beckham is the spokesmodel. A number of fashion brands, such as Ralph Lauren and Dolce & Gabbana, produce underwear to extend their branding and market ranges. However, it is one thing to extend an already existing fashion line to include underwear, but it is riskier to start a new brand based solely on underwear. Ginch Gonch is taking that chance.

The Birth of an Underwear Company

Jason Sutherland launched the Ginch Gonch brand in 2004. The name of the company comes from the Canadian slang words for underwear (sometimes referred to as knickers in Britain), *ginch* and *gonch*. Although the original conceptual goal of the company was to focus on men's underwear, it has branched out into women's and children's as well.

The company started out as a fun protest against boring, black and gray, high-priced, and poorly constructed underwear that was dominating the men's market. On a vacation in Thailand, Sutherland purchased a pair of designer underwear that sold for $60. After one washing they shrank so much that they went up his butt. He was thoroughly disgusted.

Instead of looking at this mishap as a total loss, he decided it was an opportunity. Sutherland decided he would address the issue by designing and manufacturing a better product. However, it would be totally different and reflect his personal convictions of creativity, style, and sexual freedom, as well as evoking a fun attitude for adults that reflected the carefree attitudes of kids.

Two years later, Ginch Gonch became one of the most unique and hippest premium lifestyle brands competing in the fashion underwear market. The product line is reminiscent of the Underoos brand introduced by Fruit of the Loom in the 1970s. For those who do not recall the brand, these sets of children's underwear mimicked the costumes of characters such as Superman, Wonder Woman, Princess Leia, and Luke Skywalker. The Ginch Gonch designers took that basic concept and ran with it (Figure 10.1). Ginch Gonch allows adults to relive the fun that they had as kids with their designs of men's, women's, and children's underwear. Using quality fabrics, Ginch Gonch has taken the concept of Underoos and elevated it to a moderate high-end market

A wonderful benefit of wearing Ginch Gonch underwear is its exclusivity in the fashion market. Following the traditional seasonal fashion calendar of autumn, winter, spring, and summer,

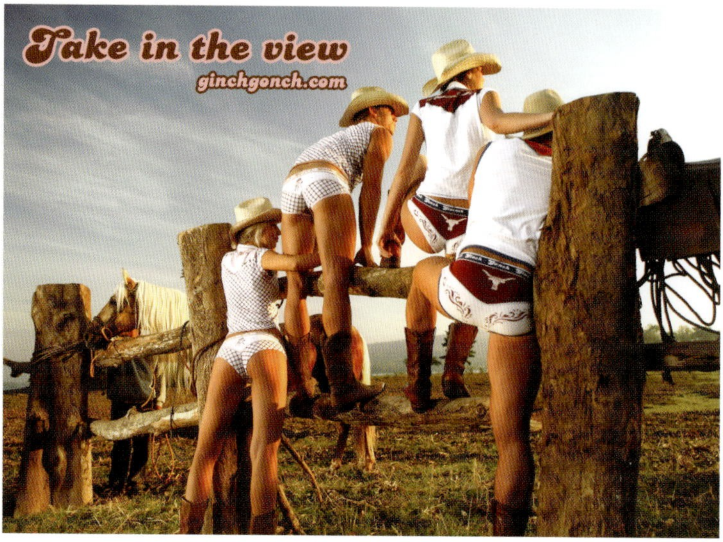
Take in the view
ginchgonch.com

FIGURE 10.1 From the "Take in the view" advertising campaign.

Ginch Gonch generally releases four collections a year, with six brief styles per collection. The underwear designs are witty, flirty, and just plain fun. Additionally, to reflect the premium underwear market, the briefs are made from the highest quality cotton and Lycra. The cuts and designs for men are based on tried-and-true styles: tighty-whiteys, Y-fronts, and bikini briefs. Like most brands, Ginch Gonch briefs have elastic waistbands with the company logo woven in and subtle trim along the top. This ultracomfortable underwear sets the standard for everyday comfort.

One would think that a line of underwear this fun would be geared toward the mass market, but that is not Sutherland's plan. He keeps the brand very exclusive. Each piece is collectible because each style is discontinued after one year. By manufacturing a limited amount of each product, the company has already garnered a reputation in the fashion world for its collectible and provocative designs.

Ginch Gonch products are sold at retailers such as Selfridges, Holt Renfrew, House of Fraser, David Jones, El Corte Inglais, and Kitson in cities from New York to Düsseldorf, and the list is still growing.

Keeping the Company Fun!

The fun style of the company's product line is reflected in Sutherland's company philosophy:

> Ginch Gonch has revitalized the underwear industry by setting trends for your rear end and regardless of your shape or size, giving you the courage to dress and undress. Quickly becoming a leader within the undie industry, GG will continue to celebrate sexual awareness and confidence in its funky flamboyant fashion concepts and in-your-face marketing campaigns. The company has always embodied the spirit of free thinking, encouraging people to embrace their motto, "Live Like a Kid." GG celebrates the kid inside all of us, with apparel designed to put a smile on your face—and your playmate's. Giving you the opportunity to wear your confidence, GG is your get-lucky, feel-lucky underwear—you can dress or undress. To top it off, it is the most comfortable underwear in your drawer, and flatters (not flattens) you in all the right places.[4]

And they do live like kids at Ginch Gonch Fashion Ltd. Sutherland does not refer to himself as the president of the company, but rather as the director of stitches and inches. The other company officers include: director of duties and cuties, director of fun and buns, and a director of production and seduction. This team ensures that the design, production, sales, and distribution of Ginch Gonch underwear all run smoothly and in a fashion that reflects fun and excitement. Sutherland exudes joy and playfulness and is genuine and refreshing.

The Ginch Gonch website (www.ginchgonch.com) is a fun place to visit. In the recent past, the company has featured international frolics such as the Wedgie Contest, in which customers submitted photos and videos of themselves either receiving or wearing a wedgie or performing a wedgie on someone else. During this wedgiemania, visitors to the website were allowed to cast their votes for the best wedgie by filling out the personal information fields and signing up for the website and newsletter. The eventual winner of the wedgie contest received $5,000 and wedgie celebrity status. The company also sponsors a model search on Canadian television station OUTtv, called *COVERguy*. The goal of the show is to find the perfect male model. Contestants are both gay and straight, and the winner receives a modeling contract with Ginch Gonch. The show is a huge hit with the gay community as well as with straight women.[5]

A Niche Market

In a 2006 interview, Sutherland revealed that when Ginch Gonch was launched it was an instant success with the gay community. "We own the gay market. . . . Gay men love them (GG underwear); lesbians love them."[6] That same year, *Out* magazine called the brand "this year's hottest underwear."[7] Ginch Gonch has shown its appreciation to the gay community by sponsoring events and attending many gay-related functions. In March 2006, the company sponsored a fundraiser for Cutting Edges, Western Canada's only gay men's hockey team.

Ginch Gonch also realizes they have a strong female following. Sutherland believes that women take bigger chances with fashion and because of this have really enjoyed the unique style of the brand. Sutherland tells of an incident in Vancouver that illustrates this enthusiasm. He parked the Ginchmobile (a van with a huge Ginch Gonch ad on the side) outside a restaurant with a glass storefront. As Sutherland entered the restaurant a table of women stood up and saluted him by dropping their jeans to reveal their Ginch Gonch underwear.[8] Many women respond to the elements of fun, freedom, and edgy expression, as well as the premium quality of Ginch Gonch products. The brand is a refreshing change in a fashion category that is sometimes taken too seriously.

Sutherland acknowledges that it is the gay market and his savvy female customers that drive his unique form of advertising. The provocative cowboy theme the company used during their "Grab Your Bulls" campaign has been looked upon by some in the marketing world as sheer genius (Figures 10.2 and 10.3).[9] Sutherland never expected such success. The popularity of the brand's cowboy theme was due in part to the Oscar-winning movie *Brokeback Mountain*. And Sutherland's inspired decision to invest in running two ads, with one geared to the straight community (see Figure 10.2) and the other directly targeted at the gay market (see Figure 10.3), was the clincher.

Sutherland doesn't care in the least that some members of the public might find direct gay marketing offensive. These ads are about personal expression and freedom. Ginch Gonch ads signify

FIGURE 10.2 The "Grab your bulls" ad that focused on the heterosexual market.

FIGURE 10.3 The "Grab your bulls" ad that focused on the homosexual market.

this ideology both in written word and visual spectacle, creating a connection with human emotions through original marketing and innovative ideas that push the boundaries of traditional apparel branding and advertising. Such forward advertising has helped this company to create a niche for itself as the "brat" of the industry. Whereas brands such as Calvin Klein allude to sexuality in their advertising campaigns, the goal of Ginch Gonch is to put it right "in your face."

INTERVIEW

Are There Gay Fashion Brands? Talking with Shaun Cole

Gay men are often stereotyped as fashion leaders. With television shows like *Queer Eye for the Straight Guy* and *Project Runway*'s Tim Gunn, homosexuals are seen as the gatekeepers of style, judges of creative clothing techniques, and how to appear *just right*. But is it all true? Do gay men have style secrets that only "come out" when they are asked their expert advice? Shaun Cole is an expert on gay men and fashion. He has worked at the Victoria and Albert Museum in London and has authored three books: *Don We Now Our Gay Apparel*, *Dialogue: Relationships in Graphic Design*, and a forthcoming book on men's underwear. He is currently the research fellow at the Centre for Fashion, the Body, and Material Cultures, University of the Arts in London. He is the man behind the secrets of gay men, their grooming habits, and their preferred brands.

Do you think that a "gay fashion" genre exists?

Yes, I do. Gay men have traditionally shown an interest in their appearance and the latest developments in clothing and fashion. The menswear revolution of the 1960s can be partly attributed to the purchasing power and stylistic statements of gay men. Gay men have also traditionally been involved in the fashion industry, as designers, stylists, and retailers. This has inevitably had an influence on other gay men's dress choices and also on straight men's choices and the fashion industry. When I am discussing the subject, I like to talk about gay style, as I feel that gay men have and are setting trends, but not necessarily meaning to be "fashionable." Traditionally, gay men's choice of clothing was about hiding or secretly signifying their sexual preference; this progressed to a much more active, visible, proud declaration of sexuality. I find it very interesting that when homosexuality and gay men are discussed (albeit briefly) in histories of fashion, it is usually in the context of a disavowal of the notion that all men interested in fashion are gay. This is of course true, but I think that the tone has been such that it implies that there is something "wrong" with gay men being interested in fashion, that it somehow taints fashion for straight men.

Do gay men prefer certain fashion brands to others? Do gay men respond to brands that advertise toward their market?
Yes, I think there are definite trends in the preference by gay men of certain brands and labels of clothing. Designers such as Jean Paul Gaultier, Dolce & Gabbana, and DSquared definitely have an appeal for gay men, through their body conscious and overtly sexual designs. I think many gay men are prepared to take a greater risk with their appearance and also (and I know this sounds like a cliché) very often have a greater disposable income to allow them to buy more expensive and exclusive designs. I think many gay men are proud to be ahead of mainstream fashions and want to have clothing that is more exclusive. For example, for a long time gay men who were traveling to the United States and responding to the Abercrombie &

Fitch sexy homoerotic advertising and branding almost exclusively wore A&F in the United Kingdom. Since A&F opened its first store in London, there has been a noticeable decline in gay men wearing the brand. The same was true of Levi's 501s in the late 1970s and early 1980s, when gay men were traveling to the gay "mecca" cities of New York and San Francisco and buying the clothes that they saw out and proud sexy American gay clones wearing on the streets and in the clubs. I think that gay men respond to clever advertising that is aimed at them. I don't think that just stating that the brand is intended for gay men is enough. I think there needs to be a greater subtlety in the way in which the brand targets gay men. There needs to be an understanding of the complexity of contemporary gay life and that while a simple image of a sexy semi-naked man might work (it certainly did for many years for Calvin Klein, who may not have been directly targeting gay men, but were certainly aware of their appeal to gay men) there needs to be a greater depth and perhaps an element of humor and insider knowledge that might not be immediately apparent to a non-gay viewer or consumer.

Do you think the so-called metrosexual movement has led the younger generation to have different views about being fashionable?

The term metrosexual has become shorthand for heterosexual men who are interested in their appearance, undertake grooming regimes (previously deemed feminine), and are avid consumers of clothing and beauty (grooming is the less feminine-identified word that is often used) products. Initially, I think the term (coined by British journalist Mark Simpson) did allow straight men that were perhaps not confident enough to buy clothes and moisturize their faces without a justification and means of approval, to undertake these increasingly popular practices and pastimes. It was also, I believe, a way for women to encourage their menfolk to take better care of themselves. A really important factor in the acceptance of the metrosexual lifestyle for many men has been the association of metrosexual celebrity role models. Heterosexual football (soccer) player David Beckham was the first metrosexual (as mentioned by Simpson in his article for Salon.com), and his sporting prowess countered the seeming effeminacy of interest in fashion and grooming. The self-confession of metrosexuality of men such as sports talk show host Mike Greenberg and actor Dominic Monaghan, and the naming of men such as actor Jude Law and television and radio host Ryan Seacrest as metrosexual by the media has had an impact. It is interesting to note that there has been a backlash against the metrosexual and his type, and the conception of new masculine types such as the ubersexuals, who embrace traditional aspects of masculinity.

The Use of Double Entendre

Ginch Gonch ads use what is known as *double entendre*, something that conveys two meanings, one of which is sexual or risqué.[10] Ginch Gonch styles not only serve a function with good garment design, but each one has a hedonic meaning attached. Cheeky taglines are written for each style, for example, "Tame Your Flame in Firetrucks," "Pop-A-Wheelie in Crotch Rockets," "Be Baad in Blue Bandana," "Harness Your Inner Outlaw in Red Bandana," and "Get Fully Loaded in Nice Guns."

Another unique advertising concept was the Ginch Gonch Holiday 2007 campaign (Figure 10.4) in which a group of models is nestled around a Christmas tree. All of them are nude except for strategically placed Ginch Gonch ribbons. The underwear for this ad is featured along the walls of the room. This image sug-

FIGURE 10.4 The 2007 "Ginch is Stealing Christmas" ad.

gests that Ginch Gonch considers its products to be works of art, which reflects their notion of collectibility. The Web address, ginchgonch.com appears across the top of the ad. Double entendre comes into play with the phrase "Ginch is stealing Christmas" in the lower right corner, which brings to mind the holiday story *How the Grinch Stole Christmas*. The double entendre is created by the phrase that has meaning for the company Ginch Gonch as well as the Dr. Seuss children's classic. This connection to the book reflects Sutherland's marketing ideology of fun and nostalgia, but with a twist.

Two more examples of double entendre are found in Figures 10.1 through 10.3. Figure 10.1 includes the phrase, "Take in the View, ginchgonch.com." The double entendre in this ad is which *view* we should take in—the landscape or the models' rear ends? Figures 10.2 and 10.3 state "Grab your bulls, Ginch Gonch," the double-meaning of which is readily apparent.

Although traditional advertising is very important for the Ginch Gonch brand, they also utilize viral fashion branding. And what better way to advertise underwear than with two live mod-

FIGURE 10.5 The Ginch Gonch boys, Benjamin Bradley (*left*) and Ethan Reynolds (*right*), made a great team

els. So, when Sutherland realized that he had a huge gay target market, he hired two "out and proud" male models.

The Ginch Gonch Boys

Benjamin Bradley and Ethan Reynolds (Figure 10.5) are the Ginch Gonch boys. Reynolds came from a traditional collegiate background, as a student at the University of Nevada. Bradley had been a pornographic film star.

In 2006, both men were recruited to be the faces of the Ginch Gonch brand. And it was a total success. The two men toured the world attending various openings and parties in nothing but their Ginch Gonch underwear. Bradley's connections in the film industry led some production companies to feature Ginch Gonch products. This, combined with the fact that his films were seen in the gay community, meant increased sales for Ginch Gonch.

Reynolds is not only a male model, but an extensive blogger. In 2006, he was the cover iGuy of *Instinct* magazine, which featured an interview about his new blog, www.bratboy school.com. In the interview, Reynolds discussed how blogs build communities and allow individuals to promote themselves to a larger audience.[11] Therefore, by creating BratBoySchool he was immediately able to reach a large portion of the gay community (and even more so after his cover photo and interview in *Instinct*). When he eventually signed on as a Ginch Gonch model, Reynolds announced his new position on the blog, which meant that Ginch Gonch would reach the individuals who subscribed to the website.

Eventually, Reynolds and Bradley began to date. This made them a bigger hit as promoters of the brand. The gay community was thrilled to see to an attractive couple promoting such a hit in the fashion community. However, in 2007, the couple split up and began to work on other projects. Bradley continues to promote Ginch Gonch products.

Never Grow Up!

Ginch Gonch is the story of an underwear company that went from being an idea to a global retailer in just a short time. By taking chances with a unique product line, creating risqué advertising, and being loyal to an established market niche, this brand has grown larger each year. How does Ginch Gonch differ from other underwear brands? It makes the whole process fun and shocks the customer with its use of double entendres. The company keeps the customer guessing about what will be next. Also, by limiting its manufacturing of each season's product line, the company makes its merchandise collectible.

Some may argue that using nudity in advertising or hiring ex-pornographic models is wrong and immoral, but that is not our decision to make. As consumers, when we find brands that personally offend, we can make the decision not to buy them. And Jason Sutherland wouldn't want "those people" as his customers anyway. What is wonderful about this brand is that it has taken global risks! Ginch Gonch is not afraid to be who it wants to be . . . and to *live like a kid*!

Discussion Questions

1. What key characteristics of Ginch Gonch's advertising makes them unique? Why do you think consumers buy Ginch Gonch products?
2. Do you think it is ethical to use sex to sell products? Can you think of other retailers who do this? How does it make their products more desirable?
3. Why do you think Jason Sutherland decided to market to the gay community? Do you think there are a lot of gay consumers? Why?
4. If you were in charge of Ginch Gonch's next fashion assortment what would you call it? Why?

Exercise

You have been hired by a fashion consultant to help solve an argument between a social morality group and the Ginch Gonch marketing department. The morality group feels that Ginch Gonch should not be allowed to have a billboard of their new advertisement next to a major freeway and 100 yards from a high school. However, the marketing team at Ginch Gonch feels they are within their rights to market their products anywhere they want. You job is to discuss the pros and cons of each side and make a decision on what should happen.

CHAPTER ELEVEN

TREATING PEOPLE RIGHT

BILLY BLUES

Hitting Below the Waist

I am a cargo pants and cargo shorts junkie! I am addicted to finding the latest and greatest styles that are available each year. Cargo pants and shorts have been around since the early 1940s and were primarily worn for their functionality. Then in the mid-1990s everyone started wearing them.[1] Some people even wear cargos as an alternative to carrying a purse or to sneak snacks into the local movie theater.

Few luxury fashion companies sell fashion-forward women's cargo-styled bottoms that are unique, fun, and exciting. But one company that does this while also focusing on fit, quality, and customer service is billy blues. It treats its customers like gold and practice socially responsible manufacturing practices on multiple fronts. The billy blues clothing line is manufactured entirely in the United States, where the company can ensure adequate working conditions for its seamstresses and ethical employment practices throughout the organization. These characteristics define billy blues and have made this brand a cult favorite among women (and some men) who literally cannot survive without them.

Who Is billy blues?

Established in 1992, billy blues is a leading contemporary women's wear company that creates stylish and comfortable women's clothing. Currently, billy blues can be found at Fred Segal Santa Monica and Nordstrom, as well as more than 800 upscale boutiques across the United States. Known for its style and fit, billy blues is a favorite among celebrities. Those who avidly purchase billy blues include Keri Russell, Alanis Morrisette, Katie Couric, Jillian Barberie, Danielle Steele, Gwen Stefani, and Lisa Kudrow, to name a few. The company has been featured in fashion magazines, such as *Cosmopolitan, Vogue, Glamour, Health, Moda, Elle, Lucky, Real Simple, Fitness,* and *YM*. The company is headquartered in Los Angeles, California, with a showroom in the New Mart.

The company founders, Billy Curtis and Reneé Thomas (Figure 11.1), are completely loyal to their customers. The team's goal is to provide women with the perfect pair of fashion-forward pants. And no one would expect anything less; the billy

FIGURE 11.1 Reneé Thomas and Billy Curtis, founders of billy blues.

FIGURE 11.2 Pieces from the Fall 2007 (left) and Spring 2008 (right) collections.

blues line ranges anywhere from $180 to almost $300, and the "private blue label" stretch khakis are about $108.

The company spares no expense when it comes to design, quality control, and production. Reneé and Billy agree that to win over customers you have to show them that you care about your product. That is why Reneé designs everything herself and monitors all in-house and contracted factories that produce billy blues products. Her design philosophy and fantastic instincts for styling women's bottoms is evident in every piece of billy blues apparel. Reneé uses high-end fabrics and details that offer stylish clothes for women of all sizes and shapes. No two styles at billy blues are alike and each garment signifies the company's brand message of contemporary sportswear elegance and style (Figure 11.2). As she pointed out in a 2007 interview, "No one buys anything basic from us."[2] The customers for this product want the perfect fit. Renée intends to expand the company further with the Private Blue Label line of moderately priced pieces.

Reneé is the president of billy blues. Born and raised in California, she studied fashion design and merchandising at Orange County College. She started her career in junior fashions, working in the design, sales, and merchandising departments for a variety of fashion companies such as GUESS, Paris Blues, Yes, and Switch. Before launching billy blues, she was a designer for Curtis/Powers, a private label clothing company that sold juniors fashions to Maurice's, Nordstrom, Macy's Wet Seal, Contempo Casuals, Miller's Outpost, Pacific Sun, Urban Outfitters, and other major department and retail stores.

Billy, the cofounder and chief executive officer of billy blues, was born and raised in Los Angeles, California. He graduated from UCLA with a degree in kinesiology. He began his career in fashion as an apprentice to Duke Boyd of Hang Ten and Lighting Bolt surf clothes. Starting at the bottom of the company, he eventually became a key executive at the firm. Billy is known for his expansion of surfing clothes into the inland states and nonsurfing areas. Billy met Reneé when she was at Curtis/Powers. Billy serves as head of sales for the company and oversees all business and financial dealings. Leaving all designing and in-house operations decisions to Reneé, he controls the external concerns of the company; dealing with vendors, going to trade shows, e-mailing customers, and scouting out new opportunities. Since cofounding the company with Reneé, he has helped position billy blues as a leading fashion company. It has been his ability to sell that has allowed the team to feature billy blues products in Fred Segal and Nordstrom.

Smart, fun, and dynamic, the billy blues team demonstrates the genius for doing business the way it should be done. They have attained success while being mindful of the company's customers as well as its social responsibility.

Ethical Production

Reneé and Billy strongly believe in the ethical treatment of workers. They know that there are less expensive manufacturing choices abroad, but have decided to keep production at home in the United States. The team has visited Asia and believes that the quality of production for both worker and product is better in the United States. Their stance is simple. They follow government policies with regard to their workers and the environment, and support all human rights legislation with regard to compensation and production. Unfortunately, their goal to produce their garments in an environmentally sound manner has been more difficult to achieve.

Consumers have expressed that they want both quality fashion apparel *and* to support the environment. What they don't know, however, is that small companies like billy blues struggle to find sources and vendors who use ethical and sustainable methods. It is a vicious cycle that every brand interested in Green production encounters. Reneé explained, "I think it (the Green movement) is great. We looked into doing it but because we are a domestic company, we have had a really hard time because the resources are hard to get. There are very few garment dye houses in L.A. that we have found [who use] natural dyes."[3] In other words, it is nearly impossible to support the movement when the rest of the industry does not. However, where the billy blues' founders are able to make a big difference is in production and the treatment of workers. Reneé and Billy firmly believe that if they treat people right they will have more success, and their company will continue to grow.

Reneé and Billy follow the production of the billy blues prod-

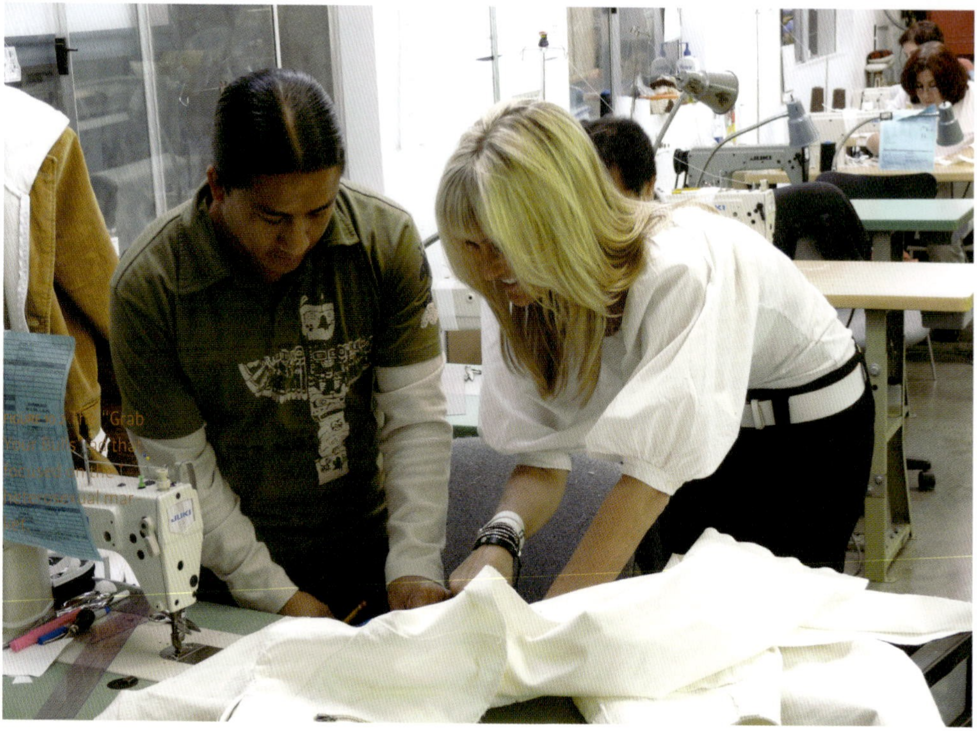

FIGURE 11.3 Reneé works with an employee constructing the latest billy blues bottoms.

uct line in each factory from start to finish. Because of Reneé's obsession with the perfect fit, she stays on top of all manufacturers who are making garments for the company. This micromanagement has allowed her to choose who will sew billy blues products. She makes it clear that every factory contracted by billy blues must meet its standard of excellence.

When she is not designing for the next season's line, Reneé is working with employees at factories; she monitors how each garment is made, ensuring that it meets every specification. She knows each of her employees personally, and feels that they are an integral part of the company. This loyalty results in dedication from her employees; many of whom have worked with Billy and Reneé for years. Reneé is certain that empowering her employees to take an active role in the business will lead to even greater success for the company (Figure 11.3); workers have a personal stake in the ultimate luxury product they help to create. After all, in the eyes of billy blues, you get what you pay for, and it knows its customers are paying for a high-quality garment.

A Consumer Cult

The customer is the most important person to billy blues. Whether it is a vendor that carries its product or an individual who wears billy blues fashions, each is treated the same. When this team talks customer service, they mean it! Even today, Billy personally answers all e-mails from customers who cannot find billy blues in local stores. Hands-on distribution is what allows this small company to compete with giants like Marc Jacobs, Moschino, Chanel, Dolce & Gabbana, and other luxury lines. The billy blues label has an exclusive brand image and plans to maintain an edge in the market.

Billy tells a story about a woman who went to a local boutique that had carried the line and discovered that they no longer had billy blues. The line was her favorite, and she was obsessed with the fit. Very upset, she went to the website and e-mailed the company. Billy immediately called the customer and told her that he would send the products she wanted to the local store. He then called the buyer who had previously bought the line and told her that one of billy blues good customers wanted to purchase billy blues pants but could not find them. He told the buyer he would personally send the customer's order to the store and she could purchase them there. The buyer was so impressed with Billy's customer service that she made the decision to start stocking the product again in all its stores.

Other vendors are just as impressed with this team. Billy and Reneé treat small boutiques with the same courtesy and kindness that they show to their nationally known clients, such as

Nordstrom and Fred Segal. Billy believes that when a small boutique writes an order for $3,500-worth of products, it is just as important as a large company's $20,000 order. Moreover, he explains that he and Reneé actually do earn a great living and have over 800 small customers nationwide. "We like working with small boutiques in every city; we don't want our product to be all over the place. Our customer doesn't want to see herself coming and going," states Billy.[4]

The team protects the company's luxury image and exclusivity by ensuring proper distribution across the nation. If one boutique is carrying billy blues, another down the block may have a completely different product assortment. "If we tell our boutique owners what their competition may have and suggest other products that are different, we find they really enjoy doing business with us. A satisfied retailer is our goal."[5]

billy blog

Billy and Reneé have set up a fashion blog on their website (www.mybillyblues.com) for their customers to post comments about the pants. The response has been fantastic. Not only has the entire staff at billy blues enjoyed reading the comments, they have learned a lot about their customers; for example, some are men! Other testimonials from customers include comments like the following:

> I love my billy blues! Slowly they have become the only pant line in my closet. One of the main reasons for this is the consistency in the fit. If I like the style on the hanger, I know the fit will be great and I can always be sure that a size 0 will fit. No need to even try the pants on! I was in the garment industry and have an understanding of how difficult this kind of consistency is to master in each collection!

YOU DO IT EVERYTIME! (Audra, design consultant, San Diego, CA)

Hi, I am so glad I discovered these pants and now I buy them whenever I can. I have never had a brand of pants that consistently fits the same and I think they are flattering and slimming. I wish they were available in more stores where I live. Actually, I feel ALL stores should carry your pants. I love them! THANKS!!! (Diane, VA)

I purchased a pair of your wide leg trousers at Nordstrom's prior to the holidays. I love the fit, style, and price point. I get so many compliments, every time that I wear them—everyone asks where I got them. They are very slimming with a lot of style. Now I want a pair of blue jeans in the same style FS103. Hopefully, I will be able to find the same style in jeans. Great design—I will be purchasing a lot of billy blues in the future!!! (Patty, Sales Director, Troy, MI)

Some of the comments have even come from retailers:

I am one of the first retailers to carry billy blues and am extremely proud to be with them since the beginning. The product is one of the top five garments in my store—it is relaxed, it is easy, and everybody loves it. And as good as their products are, they are just as great to work with. I can get special orders and reorders with no problem and there are never any shortages on shipping. Bottom line, I just love billy blues.[6] (Pam Katz, Boutique Owner, Philadelphia, PA)

Some customers are desperate to find a specific pair of billy blue pants from a previous selling season. When that happens,

Billy and Reneé respond with the best business practice ever—they make a pair for the customer. This has created a loyal following that is unparalleled in the business of ready-to-wear. With customer service at a premium, the cult seems to be growing and nothing is going to stop Billy and Reneé from sharing their passion for a luxury pair of pants.

Luxury Redefined

At a time when almost all companies are cutting costs by manufacturing overseas, billy blues continues to manufacture exclusively in the United States. Billy and Reneé direct a team of talented people who are determined to get it right, carefully controlling quality through each step of the process until billy blues land safely in specialty stores around the country. They create a luxury garment and maintain a unique edge that allows them to compete with mass luxury brands such as Chanel, Marc Jacobs, and Dolce & Gabbana. The uniqueness and exclusivity of billy blues products are what make them a luxury. The billy blues team is well on its way to creating the perfect garment of the future, selling exclusive and special pants for customers who appreciate them.

Discussion Questions

1. Why is billy blues so successful? What are some of the key business practices that the company uses to keep individuals and companies buying its products?
2. Do you think billy blues treats its customers and employees well? If so, how does billy blues demonstrates customer loyalty where other companies may miss the mark?
3. Why do you think billy blues manufactures its product in the United States while other companies have gone overseas? Do you think this is a good business practice? Why or why not?
4. What do you think the future of the company will be? What is

billy blues doing right now to expand its business? Do you think this is a smart decision? Why or why not?

Exercise

Find a brand that is socially responsible. What does it do to demonstrate this? And how have its customers responded to its business practices?

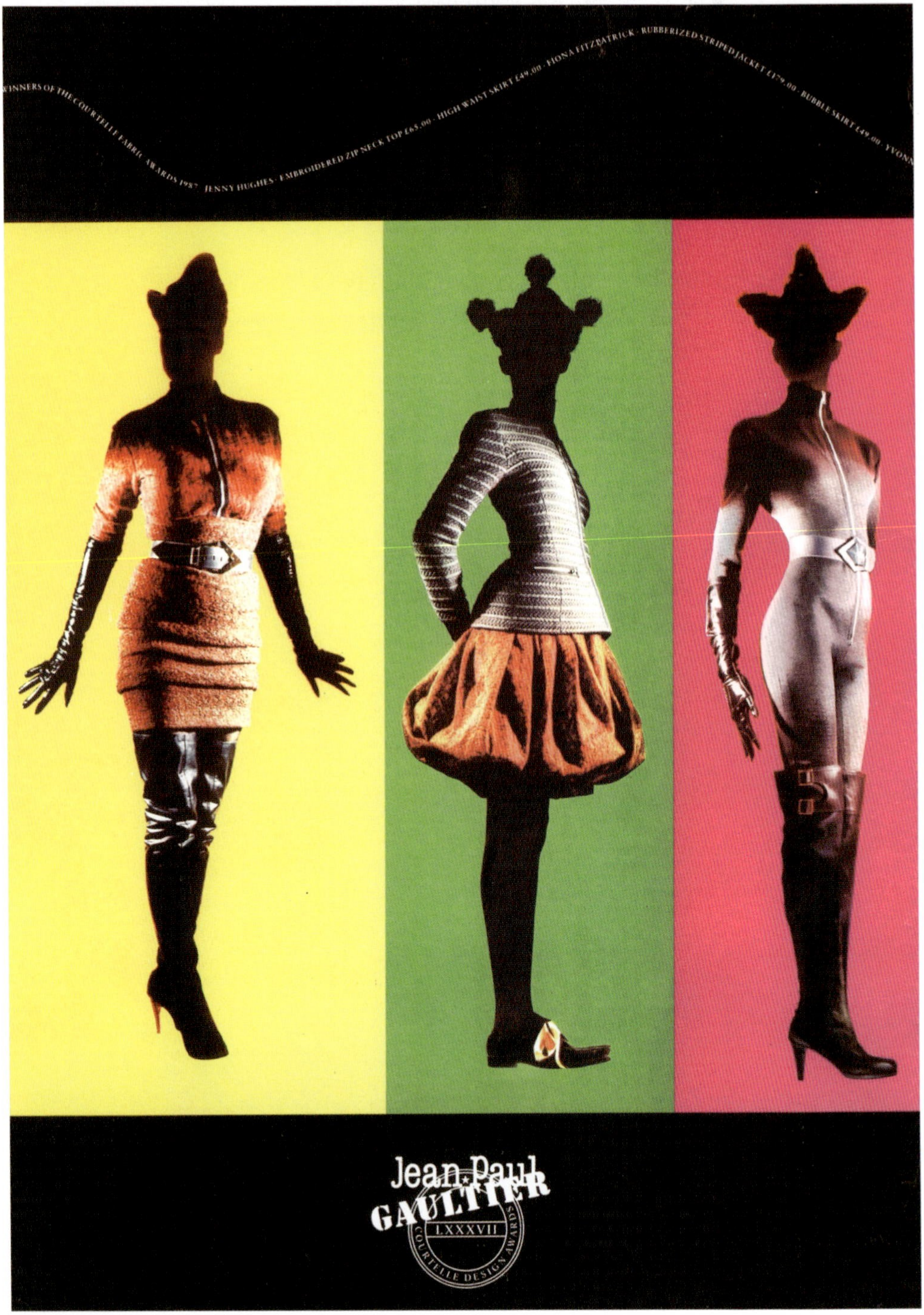
WINNERS OF THE COURTELLE FABRIC AWARDS 1987 JENNY HUGHES · EMBROIDERED ZIP NECK TOP £65.00 · HIGH WAIST SKIRT £49.00 · FIONA FITZPATRICK · RUBBERIZED STRIPED JACKET £179.00 · BUBBLE SKIRT £49.00 · YVONN
Jean Paul
GAULTIER
LXXXVII
COURTELLE DESIGN AWARDS

CHAPTER TWELVE

CONCLUSION

THE FUTURE OF FASHION BRANDS

Looking into the Crystal Ball

The fashion industry uses a variety of methods to create messages that will push the public's buttons. The stories conveyed through branding cause an emotional response in the marketplace and, ultimately, individuals identify with the brand. Consumers are made to feel special when they purchase a limited edition Johnny Cupcakes T-shirt or treat themselves to a pair of glittery Dolce & Gabbana high-heeled shoes. Attention to detail and customer satisfaction make billy blues a real find, and the double entendre in the latest Ginch Gonch advertisement always turns heads. All of these reactions are responses to company brands.

Leading professionals in the field agree that fashion branding will increase in importance as consumer goods and fashion markets become more homogenous through globalization. Logos, distinguishing characteristics, great advertising, merchandising, and even thorough employee training are going to be crucial for the survival of mass fashions. Many small companies such as Johnny Cupcakes, Ginch Gonch, and billy blues have found that creating a limited amount of a specific product makes it a "new luxury," and even a collector's item. This strategy has been quite successful for Chanel in the marketing of certain colors of its Le Vernis nail polish. Each year, a limited supply of some colors is made available, retailing at $20 per bottle. Because of the high demand for these colors, all department stores and specialty outlets that carry the product sell out immediately, causing massive frustration for thousands of customers. Bloomingdale's even creates a customer list that only allows customers to purchase the colors in numerical order. Many customers ask to be put on the following year's list as soon as they've bought the current limited edition! Sometimes discontinued colors or the latest color of Chanel's $20 wonder can be found selling on eBay for almost $300. What is it all about? Why does Chanel continue to sell this nail polish for only $20? Its strategy is to create a rush that eventually leads to a sellout, and the commodity becomes rare. Rarity seems to be a fashion-branding strategy that works.

Limited editions and the perception of luxury will continue to be effective strategies. More companies will also use stories that relate to lifestyle and culture; a fashion-branding method referred to as *cultural branding*.

Fashion and Cultural Branding

The lifestyle merchandising of Ralph Lauren, the wedding dresses of Vera Wang, the social responsibility of billy blues, and even the homoerotic ads of Ginch Gonch each reflect a particular culture. The concept of cultural branding was developed by Douglas B. Holt of the University of Oxford in his book *How Brands Become Icons*. Cultural branding addresses the individuality of the consumer. According to Holt, cultural branding is the future of all businesses that sell products and services to consumers.

Holt's concept of cultural branding is "derived from brands that have spun such compelling myths that they have become cultural icons." He goes on to explain:

> Cultural branding applies particularly to categories in which people tend to value products as a means of self-expression. . . . Marketers usually refer to these categories as lifestyle, image, badge, or ego-expressive products . . . managers can apply the lessons of cultural branding to any market offering that people regularly use, or else idealize as a means to improve their lives.[1]

According to Holt, cultural activists and individuals understand popular culture and subsequently develop successful brands. These brand leaders assemble cultural knowledge rather than worrying about traditional consumer research. Instead of a quantitative approach, they brand to the needs of a culture by understanding those individuals that live in the cultural context.[2] This cultural knowledge is developed in the following ways:

- Examining the role of major social categories of class, sex, gender, and ethnicity in identity construction rather than obscuring these categories by sorting people into "psychographic" groups.
- Viewing the brand as a historical actor in society.
- Viewing people holistically, seeking to understand what gives their lives meaning, rather than as consumers of category benefits.
- Seeking to understand the identity value of mass culture texts, rather than treating mass culture simply as trends and entertainment.[3]

To succeed, cultural brands must reflect an appropriate market and develop a product's identity. They must also be consistently reinvented when the marketplace changes as a reflection of popular culture. The marketplace determines the eventual success or failure of any brand.

Holt suggests looking at consumers as individuals instead of as target markets. This is the approach taken by small companies such as Brini Maxwell, Johnny Cupcakes, billy blues, Ginch Gonch, and Dante Beatrix. By examining each person's characteristics, these companies compose and evolve their brands along with changes in the marketplace. Successful fashion brands become attachments to the customer's lifestyle and create the perception that they have been personalized to each individual. As a result, the consumer does not feel like a member of a mass population, but rather as a unique individual.

The same can be true of larger companies that understand their products' historic equities—basics such as polos, khakis, jeans, and dress shirts—well enough to understand the most advantageous product positioning. For example, Ralph Lauren's various divisions (Polo at Macy's, Purple Label at Saks, Chaps at Kohl's, and American Living at JCPenney) reach into various markets, while reflecting a consistent Ralph Lauren brand message. The fashion brand images of Abercrombie & Fitch and Dolce & Gabbana have led to an international reputation for being risqué, which creates a desire in the marketplace for their products. Vera Wang has used the cultural institution of marriage to turn her company into a conglomerate that demonstrates her understanding of her target market as well as the needs of individuals.

These brands have become what Holt would call *iconic fashion brands*, which develop culturally contextual stories that consumers can understand and embrace. This is what makes them successful. Holt believes these brands accrue two complementary assets: cultural authority and political authority.

> When a brand authors myths that people find valuable, it earns the authority to tell similar kinds of myths (cultural authority) to address the identity desires of a smaller con-

stituency (political authority) in the future. Specifying the brand's cultural and political authority provides managers direction to develop myths for the brand, and allows them to rule out myths that are a poor fit.[4]

Brand/Story shows how these fashion brands have become accepted in our cultural context or marketplace. For example, Ralph Lauren and Vera Wang are established brands in our culture, but are they really the best for the particular product categories? The stories or myths that have been created about these brands seem to emphasize that they are; however, we may find consumers who feel that these companies make inferior products. Nevertheless, the brand myths and product reputations of Ralph Lauren and Vera Wang allow them to maintain a competitive edge in the marketplace. These brands are powerhouses supported by millions of consumer dollars.

INTERVIEW
Scouting and Patterning: Talking with Krista Pharr-Lowther

The future of fashion brands will be based on the industry's capability to emotionally connect with consumers. Just ask Krista Pharr-Lowther, a leading brand strategist with Limited Brands' strategic patterning services in Columbus, Ohio. She trains and leads the team in their international endeavors to find the latest and greatest in fashion brands and trends.

What is your professional background, and what do you do on an average day?

I received my BS (bachelor of science) in retail merchandising from Ohio University and an MS (master of science) in textiles and clothing from Ohio State University. I began my career as an assistant buyer at Express, then I went into planning and allocations, and finally into retail product testing. I worked for about eight years, then I took a break and went back to school for my master's. After I completed my postgraduate degree I did freelance for several years with a fashion website for a large corporation. Eventually, I was hired as the manager of strategic patterning in charge of process and planning.

As with any retail job, I don't think there is ever an average day. That means you basically never have the same day twice. Every day is something new; you can have a priority when you arrive at the office, and by 10 AM that is no longer of any importance to the company or brand, and they are totally interested in researching a completely new fashion concept or product. And no matter how high you are on the career ladder, there is always the administrative piece to the job—phone calls, e-mails, meetings, etc. But the focus of the day you won't know till it is all over.

Do you think the fashion market is becoming more competitive?

Yes, definitely, in a lot of ways. When you can get Vera Wang at Kohl's and Stella McCartney did a line for Target you'd better believe it is competitive. I think when Julia Roberts wore the vintage Valentino to the Oscars (2001) that reinvigorated that vintage is still a big player in fashion. Designer fashion has always been a lot about the label; but now with J. Lo, the Olson twins, Sean John, etc., having clothing lines, you can tell that fashion is not only for the wealthy. These celebrities are interpreting high-end fashion trends with their own personal style to sell to the average consumer.

What is scouting?

Scouting is looking in the usual places: Paris, London, Milan,

New York, Tokyo, and L.A., for innovative new fashion trends; but it is also about looking in small cities/destinations that do something really right.

What are the components of scouting and why is it important?
I would say one of the most important components of scouting is curiosity. You have to be curious about the where, why, how, etc. You have to want to do the research and think outside the box. For fashion you need to shop the furniture show to know what direction the colors are trending. Go to CES (a technical trade show) and see what is happening there. Then you have to have a vision that you can relay so that others will see your point. You need to have statistics to support what you think is happening.

Scouting is important to be able to do "next" better and faster than anyone else in the fashion market . . . you can get practically anything from anywhere if you are looking for it. For the average consumer, they wait till it comes to them, so you need to deliver a product that is timely and affordable, that is branded right with everything else in your store. It should supply something your customer wants, but did not even know she needed till she saw it.

How do you decide if a trend is important to follow?
Fortunately this is not part of my job. Whether or not it is brand-right would be up to the merchant team. They are very knowledgeable about their clients, the image they want to project, and where their brand is headed long term.

How do retailers mold trends to suit their business?
They have to know who their customers are and what they like or dislike. For example, fashion-forward boutiques can be more adventurous with colors and fabrics, cuts and styles; but

you can have the same item, watered down at mass stores for the general public.

What is patterning, and how does it help in planning future business?

Patterning is finding a store that seems to be doing what you are doing, or want to do. Maybe they are already selling a category of apparel that you are thinking about launching in your store, so you "pattern" them over several seasons or years to get a feel for how that business works. You will count SKUs (stock-keeping units), identify key items, examine when they bring in new merchandise, how do they set their floor, what are their marketing pieces, and do their fixtures work . . . all the elements of merchandising; basically the in-store brand. Patterning is very detail oriented and analytical. You will follow and report on every aspect of a store or category of merchandise in the exact same way for a period of time to see the trend. Kind of like the stock market; if you follow it long enough you begin to see the highs and lows. You can learn a lot from someone else's mistakes, as well as his or her successes. You must keep an eye on what is happening around you, and how that might influence your business or your customers' choices.

What is the future of scouting and patterning for hot brands?

They are two completely different retail concepts. I think both pieces are important to stay ahead of the competition, and retail business is highly competitive with global expansion. You need to keep looking for the fresh and new for yourself, but never let the competition take you by surprise. Retail is really a fast-paced, ever-evolving beast. It is key to know who your customers are and what exactly they are looking for from you before you can start bringing in new concepts and ideas.

The Power of Myths and Stories

Author and branding expert Laurence Vincent supports Douglas Holt's notions of brand myths and narratives (stories) to create a positive brand culture. Vincent defines a brand myth as:

> a traditional story of ostensibly historic events that serves to unfold part of the worldview of people or explain a practice, belief, or phenomenon. The occidental mythology of ancient civilizations served to explain the mysterious workings of the natural world through stories about the struggles and conquests of God and Heroes. Today, brand mythology serves a similar purpose. Scientific discovery answered many of the mysteries of the natural world, but it has not satisfactorily resolved the complex questions we have about social existence, or sense of self, and our relationship with the world at large. Brand mythology has curiously interceded. Like ancient mythology, it works through narrative devices.[5]

In his book *Legendary Brands: Unleashing the Power of Storytelling to Create a Winning Market Strategy*, Vincent highlights the success of Levi's and Nike. He reveals how each company established a brand culture through stories, creating the perception that the brands are superior. Also, each fashion brand situates itself within popular culture in the hope of becoming part of the social order and cultural context; in other words, a permanent fixture in the big scheme of the world. Can you picture a world without Levi's or Nike?[6]

Nike culturally integrates itself within each environment, wherever it has store locations, by becoming part of the city and its culture. For example, Niketown on Fifth Avenue in New York is very different from Niketown in Portland, Oregon, and the Nike display at Nordstrom is different from these. In Niketown, sneakers are organized by categories for exercise, streetwalking, mountain biking, golf, and so on, whereas at Nordstrom all the sneakers are featured in one area of the shoe department. The sneaker becomes enculturated into each city and retailer's environment as is appropriate.

According to Vincent, there are four parts of a brand narrative: plot, character, theme, and aesthetics.[7] Aesthetics includes any part of the brand that stimulates one of the five senses.

> Spectacle (what you see), song (what you hear musically), and diction (how words are constructed to convey meaning) are important elements for visual and performing arts. Brands, however, can also stimulate taste and touch, and these can be powerful devices.[8]

For example, entering an Abercrombie & Fitch or even a Victoria's Secret store environment is like entering a huge theater. You hear music, smell fragrance, touch clothes, and see all kinds of people in addition to the brand associates. Making a connection to the consumer through this sort of brand narrative is a key to success. The narrative must relate to the consumer both culturally and personally, and the consumer must develop a personal attachment to the brand based on the narrative. (Otherwise, the consumer may leave without purchasing anything.)

Vincent further states that through brand narratives, a symbiotic relationship between the consumer and the brand must occur for the consumer to identify with the brand. The brand narrative, whether experienced in a store or through an advertising campaign, must get attention and hold it, so that audience members can follow the characters used in the brand advertising and marketing campaign.[9] For example, the use of Audrey Hepburn in Gap's September 2006 advertising campaign for slim pants created a narrative that most consumers could relate to in their own lives. The consumer may have related to Gap, Audrey Hepburn, her movies, or just "her total beatnik look" from the images used in the windows and in the television commercial. Consumers unfamiliar with Audrey Hepburn might be interested enough to investigate further, and young hipsters might connect to a bygone era while reinventing "hip to fit" within their own cultural and personal contexts. This connection to Hepburn built brand recognition and created a narrative for Gap to perhaps build customer loyalty.

But sometimes words and actions are not needed; as the old saying goes, "a picture is worth a thousand words" or, for fashion branding, thousands of dollars. One brand that has been known for using a combination of few words and great photography is Calvin Klein. Since the early 1980s (see Figure 2.10), Calvin Klein ads have communicated narratives to consumers that keep them coming back for more of the company's products (Figure 12.1). Placing terrifically sculpted models in contemporary settings, Calvin Klein delivers the consistent image that has made him a fashion brand icon.

Individual Style and Branding

The success of fashion branding in the future will depend on the industry's ability to reflect an individual's style, making them

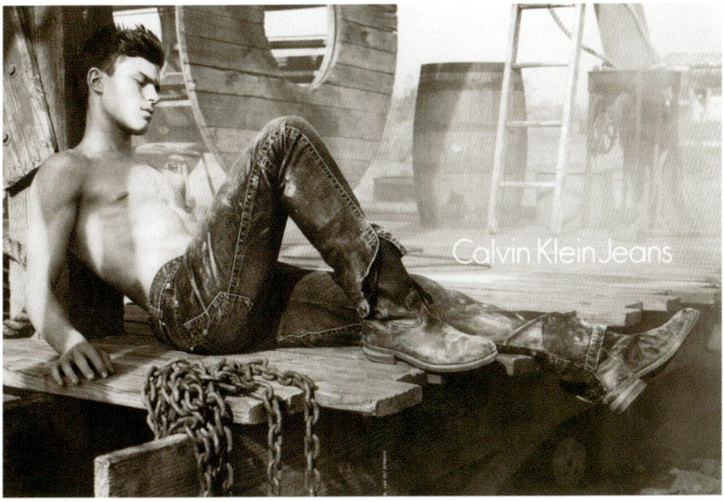

FIGURE 12.1 Calvin Klein creates visual narratives that contextualize his products in stories that allow the viewer to create their own story.

feel unique. In an article titled "Fashioning Future Fashions," scholar Gwendolyn O'Neal has noted that fashions (including all body modifications and extensions, such as tattoos and piercings) are restricted and prechosen for individuals by cultural gatekeepers (i.e., retail buyers). However, the individual decides how to blend available elements to craft a pastiche, or style, which in turn creates fashion.

O'Neal states, "Fashion does not require the creative genius of an individual which then must be endorsed by the cultural gatekeepers, but rather is a process by which individuals continually form and present themselves."[10] She further explains, "Although the body techniques and codes of conduct are imposed by external forces over which individuals have little control, the codes of conduct are acquired abilities of collective and individual practical reason." This does not remove the restrictions of the cultural context, but attaches individual fashions to a general technique of acculturation.[11]

In O'Neal's view, the acculturation process is not localized, but is cross-cultural and global. Media outlets such as telephones, televisions, computers, and other consumer electronics allow consumers immediate access to world events. Fashion trends also unfold almost simultaneously across the globe, when previously it may have taken years.

O'Neal argues that our world is commercialized and emotional, and she borrows from the futurist philosopher Rolf Jensen when she states, "It will no longer be enough to produce a useful product. A story or legend must be built into it; a story that embodies values beyond utility."[12] O'Neal believes future fashions will not be limited to objects conceived through the manipulation of creative genius to create a look or mode that is palatable to the masses. Instead, fashion will be constructed of a personal milieu in which the individual manipulates his or her own dress-body complex to create a personal mininarrative, story, or brand.

Looking to the Future

There are four key initiatives for the future of fashion branding.

- Fashion branding will continue to communicate through some method of storytelling—print media, in-store environment, the Internet, or even through store associates.
- Fashion brands will continue to create exclusive notions about their products through limited runs, unique design, and other methods of product development.
- Fashion branding will continue to create experiences that have to be physically experienced by consumers for their true essence to be understood. It cannot be experienced virtually (through the Internet), but through participant observations and ethnographic methods. *(Go outside!!)*
- Fashion branding will be about individualism.

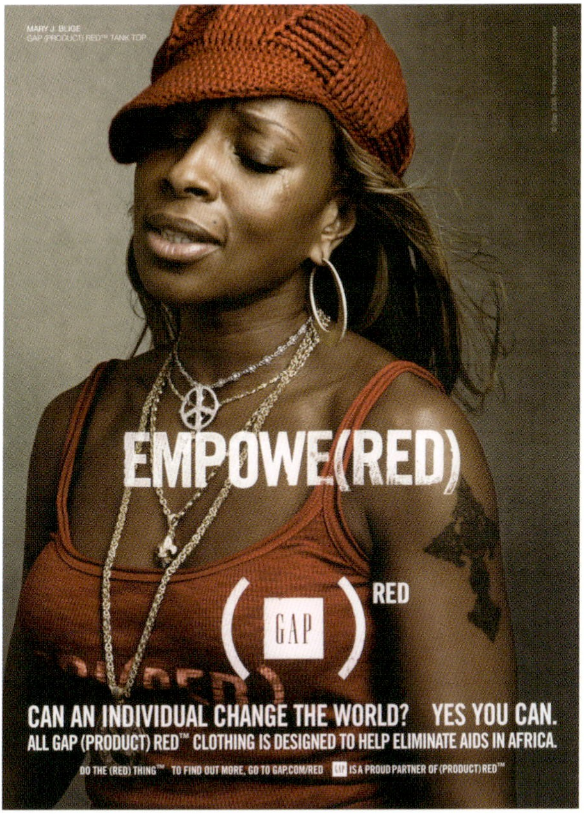

FIGURE 12.2 Gap continues to stress individuality in order to sell their merchandise. Their products are made to appear unique through associations to such stars such at as Mary J. Blige.

The latter initiative is illustrated by ads like Gap's Product(Red) campaign, featuring celebrities such as Mary J. Blige wearing their own interpretation of Gap product (Figure 12.2). Whereas this idea is not altogether new, it still stresses that individuality is a recurrent theme for branding. Gap may be reusing its branding strategy from the early 1990s (see Figure 2.8), but it is important to note that generating a theme of *individuality* to sell insignificant fashion items such as T-shirts, jeans, and khakis is an advanced branding method. And Gap is not the only retailer doing such advertising. Ralph Lauren, Abercrombie & Fitch, J.Crew, Eddie Bauer, DKNY, Diesel, Calvin Klein, Kenneth Cole, Tommy Hilfiger, Rocawear, and Sean John all use the concept of individuality and personal style to sell similar mass fashion clothes.

The Mary J. Blige ad demonstrates that mass fashions can be personalized to form a unique style. Her body modifications, such as tattoos and piercing, create a Mary J. Blige brand complex that is unique. To revisit the ideas of Gwendolyn O'Neal, this example allows us to see how Mary J. Blige uses her own personal milieu to create a new branded style. Even though retail buyers, fashion stylists, and those of cultural power have created the image, the fashions still appear new and special in the eyes of the viewer because Mary J. Blige is wearing them. A story is created, and that, my friends, is the power and the genius of fashion branding.

Discussion Questions

1. What are the ideas behind Douglas Holt's theory of cultural branding? Give examples that differ from the text.
2. How does Laurence Vincent support Douglas Holt's notions of fashion branding? Give examples that differ from the text.
3. What are Gwendolyn O'Neal's ideas about the future of fashion branding? Give examples of how you personally reflect her ideas in your own wardrobe and style.

Exercise

Find a form of fashion branding. How does this fashion branding tell a story, and how does it reflect popular culture. How do you think this fashion brand will evolve in the future? Use the theoretical ideas of this chapter to discuss this brand.

NOTES

Chapter One

1. Youn-Kyoung Kim, Pauline Sullivan, and Judith Cardona Forney, *Experiential Retailing: Concepts and Strategies that Sell* (New York: Fairchild Publications, 2007), 327–46.
2. Evelyn Brannon, *Fashion Forecasting: Research, Analysis, and Presentation,* 2nd ed. (New York: Fairchild Publications, 2005), 406.
3. Klaus Fog, Christian Dudtz, and Baris Yaka, *Storytelling Branding in Practice* (Denmark: Springer, 2005), 13–25.
4. Ibid., 23.
5. Ibid., 31.
6. Adam Adamson, *Brandsimple: How the Best Brands Keep It Simple and Succeed* (New York: Palgrave McMilllan, 2006), 181–83.

Chapter Two

1. Charles W. King, "A Rebuttal to the 'Trickle Down' Theory," in *Towards Scientific Marketing*, ed. Stephen A. Greyer

(Chicago: American Marketing Association, 1963), 108–25.
2. Childers, Joseph and Gary Hentzi, *The Columbia Dictionary of Modern Literary and Cultural Criticism* (New York: Columbia University Press, 1995), 191–92.
3. Youn-Kyoung Kim, Pauline Sullivan, and Judith Cardona Forney, *Experiential Retailing: Concepts and Strategies that Sell* (New York: Fairchild Publications, 2007), 26–27.
4. Roland Barthes, *The Fashion System* (New York: Columbia University Press, 1985), 3-18.
5. Steven Best and Douglas Kellner, *Postmodern Theory: Critical Interrogations* (New York: The Guilford Press, 1991), 119.
6. Jean Baudrillard, "The System of Objects," in *Jean Baudrillard Selected Writings*, ed. Mark Poster (Stanford, CA: Stanford University Press, 1988), 19.
7. Ibid., 170.
8. Best and Kellner, *Postmodern Theory*, 119.
9. Baudrillard, "The System of Objects," 17.
10. Ibid., 19.
11. Berger, *The Portable Postmodernist*, 87.
12. Ibid., 87.
13. Ibid., 79.
14. Ibid., 87.
15. Ibid., 5.
16. Judith Williamson, *Decoding Advertisements: Ideology and Meaning in Advertising*, (New York: Marion Boyars Publishers LTD, 2002), 12.
17. Jean A. Hamilton, "The Macro-Micro Interface in the Construction of Individual Fashion Forms and Meaning," *The Clothing and Textiles Research Journal*, 15, vol. 3 (1997): 165–71.
18. Ibid., 165.
19. Ibid., 167.
20. Ibid., 168.
21. Ibid., 263.

22. DeBord, "Texture and Taboo," 263.
23. Teri Agins, *The End of Fashion: How Marketing Changed the Clothing Business Forever* (New York: HarperCollins Publishers Inc, 1999), 14–15.
24. Marc Gobe, *Emotional Branding: The New Paradigm for Connecting Brands to People* (New York: Allworth Press, 2001), xvii.
25. Grant McCracken, *Culture and Consumption* (Bloomington: Indiana University Press, 1988), 71–89.
26. Grant McCracken, *Culture and Consumption II* (Bloomington: Indiana University Press, 2005), 162–70.
27. Ibid., 177.
28. Ibid., 178–91.

Chapter Three

1. Agins, Teri, *The End of Fashion: How Marketing Changed the Clothing Business Forever* (New York: HarperCollins Publishers Inc, 1999), 14–15.
2. Rugby, "About Rugby," www.rugby.com/about/default.aspx?ab=topnav_r_AboutRugby (accessed June 29, 2008).
3. Lauren, Ralph. *Ralph Lauren* (New York: Rizzoli, 2007).
4. Gross, Michael. *Genuine Authentic: The Real Life of Ralph Lauren* (New York: Perennial, 2003).
5. McDowell, Colin. *Ralph Lauren: The Man, the Vision, the Style* (New York: Rizzoli, 2003).
6. Ibid., 15.
7. Gross, *Geniune Authentic*, xvii.
8. McDowell, *Ralph Lauren*, 20.
9. Birrittella, Buffy. "The Big Knot." *Daily News Record*, December 19, 1967.
10. McDowell, *Ralph Lauren*, 29.
11. Lauren, *Ralph Lauren*.
12. Ibid., 399.

13. McDowell, *Ralph Lauren*, 202.
14. Ibid.
15. Gross, *Genuine Authentic*, 170.
16. McDowell, *Ralph Lauren*, 202.
17. Lauren, *Ralph Lauren*, 409.
18. McDowell, *Ralph Lauren*, 202.
19. Lauren, *Ralph Lauren*, 410.
20. McDowell, *Ralph Lauren*, 202.
21. Ibid.
22. Lauren. *Ralph Lauren*, 417–18.
23. Ibid., 434.
24. Ibid., 437.
25. Ibid., 437.
26. McDowell, *Ralph Lauren*, 203.
27. Ibid., 203.
28. Ibid., 203
29. Ibid.
30. Ralph Lauren, "History." Ralph Lauren website, about.polo.com/history.asp (accessed January 12. 2007).

Chapter Four

1. The Biography Channel, "Dolce & Gabbana," www.thebiographychannel.co.uk/biography_story/942:1115/1/Dolce_Gabbana.htm (accessed February 14, 2008).
2. Dolce & Gabbana, "Community," www.dolcegabbana.com/ (accessed February 29, 2008).
3. Sarah Mower, *20 Years Dolce & Gabbana*. Milan: 5 Continents Editions, 2005, 20.
4. Dolce & Gabbana.
5. Ibid.
6. Commercial Closet Association, "Dolce & Gabbana/D&G," www1.commercialcloset.org (accessed February 29, 2008).

7. Mike Wilke, personal interview with author, June 13, 2008.
8. Mower, 13.
9. Ibid.
10. Ibid.
11. Dolce & Gabbana.
12. Ibid.
13. Luisa Zargani, "D&G Set to Expand Globally, Launch New Store Concept," *WWD.com*, www.wwd.com/article/print/122681 (accessed February 19, 2008).
14. Ibid.
15. Ibid.
16. Sophia Banay, "The Flush," *Condé Nast Traveler*, www.conceirge.com/ideas/styledesign/tour/detail?id=1457&page=3&print=true (accessed February 29, 2008).
17. Ibid.
18. Dolce & Gabbana.

Chapter Five

1. www.verawang.com.
2. Eric Wilson, "Vera Wang's Business Is No Longer All Dressed in White," *The New York Times*, December 15, 2005.
3. A&E Television Networks, *Fashion: Icons of Fashion*. DVD, 2001.
4. Ibid.
5. Anne Stegemeyer, *Who's Who In Fashion* (4th ed.; New York: Fairchild Books, 2004), 260.
6. A&E Television Networks.
7. Associated Press, "Vera Wang to Design Line Just for Kohl's," *USA Today*, August 24, 2006.
8. Ibid.
9. www.verawang.com

10. Emily Lung, personal communication with author, September 15, 2007.

Chapter Six

1. Abercrombie & Fitch, "Investor Relations," www.abercrombie.com (accessed on July 15, 2007).
2. Tom Reichart, *The Erotic History of Advertising* (New York: Prometheus Books, 2003), 235.
3. Laura Bird, "Beyond Mail Order: Catalogs Now Sell Image, Advice," *Wall Street Journal*, July 29, 1997, Sec B.
4. David Reines, "All the Nudes That's Fit to Print," *Nerve.com*, www.nerve.com (accessed on May 15, 2006).
5. Greg Lindsay, "Death of A&F's Quarterly: Problem Wasn't Sex But Brand's Loss of Cool," *Women's Wear Daily*, December 11, 2003.
6. Dwight A. McBride, *Why I Hate Abercrombie & Fitch* (New York: New York University Press, 2005).
7. Youn-Kyung Kim, Pauline Sullivan, and Judith Cardona Forney. *Experiential Retailing: Concepts and Strategies that Sell* (New York: Fairchild Books, 2007).
8. Ko Floor, Branding a Store: How to Build Successful Retail Brands in a Changing Marketplace (London: Kogan Page, 2006).
9. Vincent, Laurence, *Legendary Brands: Unleashing the Power of Storytelling to Create a Winning Market Strategy* (Chicago: Dearborn Trade Publishing, 2002).
10. Holt, Douglas B., *How Brands Become Icons* (Boston: Harvard Business School, 2004).
11. Meyer Sound, "Meyer Sound Loudspeakers Dress Up Audio for Abercrombie & Fitch," meyersound.com/news/2006/Abercrombie (accessed on July 15, 2007).
12. John Stevenson Gallery, "Mark Beard," (June 21, 2007).

www.johnstevenson-gallery.com/beard_2004/beard_2004_text.html (accessed on July 15, 2007).

Chapter Seven

1. Tovia Smith, "Johnny Cupcakes Finds Sweet Success in T-shirts," *National Public Radio*, August 19, 2006, www.npr.org (accessed on January 14, 2008).
2. John Earle, "The Story," www.johnnycupcakes.com (accessed on January 16, 2008).
3. Ibid.
4. Ibid.
5. Ibid.
6. John Earle, personal interview with author, April 22, 2007.
7. Ibid.
8. Smith.
9. Smith.

Chapter Eight

1. Mintel Report, "Handbags—US—May 2007," academic.mintel.com (accessed on February 12, 2008).
2. Ibid.
3. Ibid.
4. Ibid.
5. Krista Pharr-Lowther, personal communication with author, February 8, 2008.
6. Mintel Report.
7. Ibid.
8. Ibid.
9. Allison Rosen, "Pet Mania . . . Unleashed!" *TimeOut New York*, March 30, 2006, www.timeout.com/newyork/articles/features/1008/pet-maniaunleashed (accessed February 12, 2008).

10. Ibid.
11. Ibid.
12. Mintel Report, "Baby Durables—US—April 2007," academic .mintel.com (accessed on February 12, 2008).
13. Ibid.
14. Dante Beatrix, www.dantebeatrix.com/about/ (accessed on February 12, 2008).
15. Ibid.
16. "Baby Grand," *WWD Accessories* (September/October, 2004): 38.
17. Ibid.

Chapter Nine

1. George DeSoto, "Brini is Retro with a Twist," *USA Today* (January 16, 2004): D1.
2. Chris Hedges, "Part Martha Stewart, Part RuPaul," *The New York Times* (January 8, 2000): B1.
3. Ibid.
4. Ben Sander, personal interview with author, November 15, 2005.
5. Hedges, B1.
6. Amy Briamonte, personal interview with author, May 1, 2006.
7. DeSoto, D1.

Chapter Ten

1. Larissa Ardis, "Unmentionables Worth Talking About," http://northwood.ca/fall-2006/ginch-gonch (accessed January 21, 2006).
2. Mintel Report, "Men's Underwear-US- December 2006," http://academic.mintel.com (accessed on January 21, 2007).
3. Ibid.

4. Jason Sutherland, http://www.ginchgonch.com (accessed January 21, 2006).
5. OutTV, "Coverguy," www.outtv.ca (accessed February 3, 2008).
6. Ardis.
7. Ibid.
8. Ibid.
9. Ibid.
10. Michael Agnes and Andrew N. Sparks, *Webster's New World Dictionary* (Cleveland, OH: Wiley Publishing, Inc., 2004).
11. Christopher Hawkins, "Blogger Boy," *Instinct* (January 2006): 46-48.

Chapter Eleven

1. Mary L. Gavenas, *The Fairchild Encyclopedia of Menswear* (New York: Fairchild Books, 2008), 80.
2. L.D., "Sportswear News & Trends," *Fashion Markets Magazine* (August, 2007).
3. Reneé Thomas, personal interview with author, September 16, 2007
4. Billy, personal interview with author, September 16, 2007.
5. Ibid.
6. My billy blues, "Testimonials," www.mybillyblues.com/testimonials.php (accessed on January 13, 2008).

Chapter Twelve

1. Douglas Holt, *How Brands Become Icons* (Boston, MA: Harvard Business School Press, 2004), 215.
2. Ibid., 209.
3. Ibid., 210.
4. Ibid., 211.
5. Laurence Vincent, *Legendary Brands: Unleashing the Power of*

Storytelling to Create Winning Market Strategy (Chicago, IL: Dearborn Trade Publishing, 2002), 25.

6. Ibid.
7. Ibid., 123.
8. Ibid.
9. Ibid., 127.
10. Gwendolyn O'Neal, "Fashioning Future Fashion." in *Fashioning the Future: Our Future from Our Past*, eds. Patricia Cunningham and Gayle Strege (Ohio State Historic Costume & Textiles Collection, 1996), 27.
11. Ibid.
12. Ibid., 28.

CREDITS

Foreword
F.1 Courtesy of Fairchild Publications, Inc.

Chapter One
Opener Copyright Mitch Gillette/Courtesy of Modern Eye, Philadelphia, PA; 1.1 Courtesy of The Advertising Archives; 1.2 Courtesy of Coca-Cola

Chapter Two
Opener Courtesy of The Advertising Archives; 2.1 Courtesy of The Advertising Archives; 2.2 Courtesy of The Advertising Archives; 2.3 Courtesy of The Advertising Archives; 2.4 Courtesy of The Advertising Archives; 2.5 Courtesy of The Advertising Archives; 2.6 Courtesy of The Advertising Archives; 2.7 Courtesy of the author; 2.8 Courtesy of The Advertising Archives; 2.9 Courtesy of The Advertising Archives; 2.10 Courtesy of The Advertising Archives; 2.11 Courtesy of the author; 2.12 Courtesy of The Advertising Archives

Chapter Three
Opener Courtesy of The Advertising Archives; 3.1 © Frances M. Roberts/Alamy; 3.2 © Kim Karpeles/Alamy; 3.3 Courtesy of The Advertising Archives; 3.4 Courtesy of The Advertising Archives; 3.5 Courtesy of The Advertising Archives; 3.6 Courtesy of The Advertising Archives; 3.7 Courtesy of Jill Walker-Roberts; 3.8 Courtesy of The Advertising Archives; 3.9 Courtesy of The Advertising Archives

Chapter Four
Opener Courtesy of The Advertising

Archives; 4.1 Courtesy of Condé Nast Publications, Inc.; 4.2 Courtesy of The Advertising Archives; 4.3 Courtesy of The Advertising Archives; Interview Courtesy of the author; 4.4 Courtesy of The Advertising Archives; 4.5 Courtesy of The Advertising Archives; 4.6 Courtesy of The Advertising Archives

Chapter Five
Opener Courtesy of The Advertising Archives; 5.1 © Deborah Feingold/Corbis; 5.2 Courtesy of The Advertising Archives; 5.3 Courtesy of Fairchild Publications, Inc.; Interview Courtesy of the author

Chapter Six
Opener © Copyright 2003 by 20031202/Zuma Press/Newscom; 6.1 The Advertising Archives; Interview Courtesy of Bloomingdale's; 6.2 Courtesy of the author; 6.3 Courtesy of the author; 6.4 Courtesy of the author; 6.5 Courtesy of the author; 6.6 Courtesy of the author; 6.7 Courtesy of the author; 6.8 David Pomponio/FilmMagic for Paul Wilmot Communications/Getty Images

Chapter Seven
Opener Dave Green/Courtesy of Johnny Cupcakes; 7.1 Dave Green/Courtesy of Johnny Cupcakes; 7.2 Dave Green/Courtesy of Johnny Cupcakes; 7.3 Dave Green/Courtesy of Johnny Cupcakes; 7.4 Dave Green/Courtesy of Johnny Cupcakes; Interview Courtesy of Jennifer Lea Cohan; 7.5 Dave Green/Courtesy of Johnny Cupcakes; 7.6 Dave Green/Courtesy of Johnny Cupcakes

Chapter Eight
Opener Courtesy of Dante Beatrix; 8.1 Courtesy of Dante Beatrix; 8.2 Courtesy of Dante Beatrix; Interview Courtesy of Jill Walker-Roberts; 8.3 Courtesy of Dante Beatrix; 8.4 Courtesy of Dante Beatrix; 8.5 Courtesy of Dante Beatrix

Chapter Nine
Opener Bradford Noble/E! Networks/Philadelphia Daily News/KRT/Newscom; 9.1 Courtesy of Brini Maxwell; Interview Courtesy of the author; 9.2 Courtesy of Brini Maxwell

Chapter Ten
Opener Courtesy of Ginch Gonch; 10.1 Courtesy of Ginch Gonch; 10.2 Courtesy Ginch Gonch; 10.3 Courtesy of Ginch Gonch; Interview Courtesy of Shaun Richard Cole; 10.4 Courtesy of Ginch Gonch; 10.5 Courtesy of Ginch Gonch

Chapter Eleven
Opener Courtesy of billy blues; 11.1 Courtesy of billy blues; 11.2 Courtesy of billy blues; 11.3 Courtesy of billy blues

Chapter Twelve
Opener Courtesy of The Advertising Archives; Interview Courtesy of Krista Pharr-Lowther; 12.1 Courtesy of The Advertising Archives; 12.2 Courtesy of The Advertising Archives

INDEX

Page numbers in italics refer to figures.